THE M.O.S.T.

The Momentum of Success Technique

8 Powerful Shifts To Propel Your
Potential & Purpose

MR. AFFIRMATION

With The Information You
Need To Succeed

_____

_____

<u>8 Powerful Shifts To Propel Your Potential & Purpose</u>
Copyright @ 2017 by Shawn Momon

Unless otherwise indicated, all scripture quotations are taken from the *King James Version* of the Bible.

Disclaimer

The information published in this book represents the opinions, personal research, and business experience of the author. Since the success of anyone depends upon the skills and abilities of the person, the author makes no guarantees, and disclaims any personal loss or liabilities that may occur as a result of the use of the information contained herein.

This publication is designed to provide accurate and authoritative information in regard to the subject matter covered in it. It is provided with the understanding that the publisher is not engaged in rendering legal, accounting, or other professional services. If legal advice or other expert assistance is required, the services of a competent professional person should be sought.

ISBN-13: 9780692967201
ISBN-10: 0692967206

Special Thanks

Jamillah Anika Momon (My Wife)

To my wife Anika, who has been loving and supportive throughout the whole process of writing this book: I LOVE YOU SO MUCH! When it comes to my "WHY" you're at the top of the list, it's because of your unconditional love for me that fills my heart with unspeakable joy and happiness. It is the fuel that helps me to GRIND and work hard. I strive to make you proud everyday. Your prayers have given me the momentum to continue to walk in my GOD given purpose. As I launch into the deep of operating in my purpose, I know you have my back. I love sharing my life and dreams with you forever. I LOVE YOU.

David and Hannah Momon (My Children)

I thank both of you for loving me unconditionally. I see Greatness inside each of you. To my baby girl - you're so precious to me and you have so many talents that I see developing in you every day. To my little man, I got to be Great because you imitate everything I do. You have the gift of trying to figure things out, and you will discover & create new things. As I make history, you both make history with me. Daddy loves you both. It is written!!!

Special Thanks (Continued)

Pastor Ocie Reese, Jr. & First Lady Paula Reese
(Alpharetta, Georgia)

To the man and woman of God who saw potential in me that I did not see. When I first joined Anointed Word Christian Ministries (AWCM), I sat in the back of the church all alone to hear you preach with power and authority. I did this for months, until you approached me after service one day to tell me that you had been watching from a distance. You were the first person who helped me develop my leadership skills to become a better servant. I accepted the calling of being a Deacon at AWCM. Thank you for allowing me to serve you, your family, and in ministry. I am forever grateful. Like you always say, "Don't compete, don't compare, and don't complain."

Pastor T.J. McBride & First Lady Shunnae McBride
(Atlanta, Georgia)

To my Pastor and First Lady who knew just what I needed to prepare me for becoming a husband and father. I remember when I told you about proposing to my wife, you were so excited and happy for us. Your transparency about your marriage spoke volumes to me about how to love my wife and lead my family. Thank you both for all your support in my dreams and aspirations. You taught the most valuable lesson when you said, "Your blessings come from serving others." I have a servant's heart as a Deacon at Tabernacle of Praise Church International (TOPCI). Thank you and your family for always praying and guiding our family to stay closer to God.

Special Appreciation

Family- My brother Alton Momon and sister-in-law Kathy Momon (Nia, Alton Jr., and Turner); My Uncle Marvin Momon; My Uncle Jerry Glanton and Aunt Gail Glanton (Carl, Terri, Kecia, and Jerry, Jr.); My Uncle John Momon, Jr. and Aunt Euravine Momon (Sheldon and John III); My Grandmother Judy Momon (Reginald and Bernita); My nieces, nephews, cousins, other family members, and friends

In Laws- My mother-in-law Esther White and brothers-in-law Dereik White and Marlo White

Churches- Love of God Church, Anointed Word Christian Ministries, Tabernacle of Praise Church International

Jobs- Wild Pair Shoe Store, Nissan of Union City, Georgia State Mortgage, Federal Express, Publix Supermarket #1183, Media Printing, Mrs. Jamie Mann (New Horizons New Directions Preparatory Academy Staff and Students)

Schools- Venetian Hills Elementary, Therrell High School and The Great Class of 1988, Troy State University, University of Phoenix, Grand Canyon University

Fraternity- Kappa Alpha Psi Fraternity, Inc. and Theta Phi Chapter at Troy State University

Mentor- Kendall Ficklin and The Grindation Family

Dedication

I dedicate this book to the most influential woman in my life. In the 4th grade my mother spoke an affirmation that I still remember today. At that time I was on the verge of failing 4th grade math and being retained. But mother saw something in me that was greater than the problem of understanding math. My mother's affirmations were, "You will learn Math!" "You will get A's in Math!" "You will be Great in Math!"

My mother, Clarissa Momon, took time out of her schedule of working a full-time job, catching the bus to and from work, cooking meals, and being a single mother of 2 boys, plus helping me with my math. I have a vivid memory of mother and I studying math together. Through my tears, I remember hearing those affirming words in my mother's voice and then it just clicked. I started rattling off correct answers to the math questions that mother would ask. I was a quick thinker and had the ability to calculate large numbers in my head. Those affirmations stretched my mind and caused me to believe I was great. I am forever grateful for my mother's love, support, and more importantly giving me my special gift of affirmations.

I love you mom. Thanks for making us go to church when we were young. That is why I love the Lord and have faith that God has great things for me to accomplish, like writing this book.

Preface

I wrote this book to inspire and activate people to propel toward success. Personally, I had many struggles and setbacks in my life that made me sometimes want to quit. Most people want to be Successful but do not know how to get the Momentum started. This is the book you have been waiting for all your life: **The M.O.S.T. - The Momentum Of Success Technique.**

This book unfolds my life story from being unemployed to owning my own business by using Affirmations. I once was unemployed, single, and afraid to pursue my dreams. Once I tapped into the Momentum zone of applying 8 Principles, my life changed instantly. I started my own businesses, I am happily married, I have wonderful children, and I was promoted to Dean of Students.

Positivity is the *most* powerful Energy needed for the Momentum of Success. Included in this book are well over 100 of the greatest affirmations ever created because they are geared toward your mind, passion, and purpose.

I was always popular but afraid.
I have always loved God, but did not trust God totally.
I was smart but made bad decisions.
I always knew what I wanted to do,
but I did not know how to do it.
The M.O.S.T. is the Answer!!!

Foreword

By Pastor T.J. McBride

Shawn Momon has done a great job of outlining principles in this book that will change your life. One of the most important things to have in your life is a strategic plan. Because of his background as a lifelong educator, Shawn strategically has given us a plan to be successful in every area of our lives.

This book will help you discover your potential and ultimately push you into your purpose. I encourage you to read and study this book. If applied to your life, you will see tremendous results. Thank you Shawn for this awesome and timely book.

Pastor Timothy J. McBride
Founder and Senior Pastor of Tabernacle of Praise Church International in McDonough, GA.
Author of Faith for Provision & It's According to Your Faith

Table of Contents

INTRODUCTION

Although this book is titled *The M.O.S.T.*, it could also be called *The 8 Steps to the Momentum of Success,* because anyone that is successful at one point or another had to experience some type of momentum. I researched well over 100 successful people in various backgrounds and they all had 8 things in common that pushed them into their purpose and propelled their potential to success. The acronym that describes those 8 traits of being successful is M.O.M.E.N.T.U.M. These 8 shifts of momentum were always prevalent, although successful individuals may have had other traits: Mindset, Opportunity, Motivation, Enthusiasm, Networking, Time Management, Uniqueness, and Money Management. Even though life is difficult at times, people have to be careful of how they speak. This book is a basic way to use affirmations to help motivate men and women to become great in their marriages, careers, finances, and health.

In my book, *The M.O.S.T.*, I have outlined 8 steps to discover your purpose and build up your potential. From the essence of affirmations, you become what you think and speak. When you change how you think and speak, you change the results in your life. For instance, your thoughts and words can Create unlimited spiritual oneness & commitment, wealth potential & prosperity, and a healthy body & relationships.

Success in life can be defined as the continued expansion of happiness and the progressive realization of worthy goals. Momentum is the ability to fulfill desires with effortless ease. Yet momentum, including creation of wealth, has always been believed to be a process that requires hard work, and often considered to be at the expense of others. We need a more spiritual approach to momentum and affluence, which is the abundant flow of all good things to you. With the correct speech, a new mindset, and consistent action on your purpose, it becomes a magnet that attracts the things you truly desire. This book creates a blueprint for success in 8 chapters by using the concept of Triaffirmation ™ when you state the same affirmation in 3 different ways at 3 different times in a day. Also, the Triaffirmation ™ has connecting acronyms that help you to remember or associate phrases or words with the affirmation. With this unique concept of affirmations, it resets your mind to be able to destroy doubt or fear forever. With the use of Triaffirmation ™, "Success is the option."

1. MINDSET

<u>Romans 12:2 (KJV)</u> And be not conformed to this world: but be ye transformed by the renewing of your mind, that ye may prove what is that good, and acceptable, and perfect, will of God.

Mindset To Be Great

Two questions I have to ask you first:

Do you know your purpose?
Do you want to tap into your potential?

Based on you answering YES to the above questions, the first thing you must do to experience Success is to start with your mindset. The mindset is the first step in **The Momentum of Success Technique**. There has to be drastic shifts in your thinking to become a person with a winning mentality. This shift is going to require you to replace all negative thinking with positive thinking. This is how you get **The M.O.S.T.** out of your mind. God created you with a creative and innovative mind that has power beyond your belief. Your mind is full of great ideas, happy thoughts, and creative solutions to problems. Positive things flow throughout your mind. Then you can achieve "**The M.O.S.T.**" results that you desire in your life.

Positive thinking puts you in the driver's seat of your life. YOU control the direction of your life, not your circumstances. As you start to travel a new course in your life, you can set your mind on being Great. Now when you think about mindset, it means to have a mental attitude to determine how you respond or react to a particular situation. Let's compare a Negative Mindset to a Positive Mindset.

Negative Mindset:

· I want success but, I think I have missed my opportunity.

· A career change is what I really need, but I am afraid to start all over again.

· The dream of my perfect job with a great salary and benefits package is a distant memory.

· Why do less qualified people keep getting promoted on my job instead of me?

· I am afraid of getting married again because the first marriage did not work.

· Will I ever be able to pay all my bills off and have good credit?

· Can I really find my soul mate and will we live happily ever after?

· Maybe my purpose is just to have a job and pay bills?

· I have tried everything, but still have trouble losing weight.

· There are too many temptations of food and that is why I have unhealthy eating patterns.

· God knows my heart, even though I only pray when I get in trouble.

· I am too busy to go to church or read the bible.

· I want to spend time with my kids, but I need that overtime money on the weekends.

· I am so unorganized and always running late for everything.

· I have many visions but I am unclear where to start.

· I have a major problem asking for help from other people.

· I am shy and I do not like meeting new people at all.

Positive Mindset:

·I see unlimited opportunities for the success I desire.

·I am open to having a fresh start with a career change.

·My dream is my current reality of my perfect job with a great salary and benefits package.

·I deserve a promotion on my job because I am qualified.

·I desire to be married again and this time is going to be the best.

·I pay my bills on time and I have a great credit score.

·My soul mate is near and we live happily ever after.

·My purpose is to start my own business and provide a valuable service to other people.

·I exercise and I am satisfied with my weight loss.

·I eat healthier and enjoy delicious foods that are healthy.

·I pray to God throughout the day.

·I read my bible daily and I attend church regularly.

·My work schedule allows me to have weekends off so I can spend time with my kids.

·I am organized and arrive on time consistently for everything.

·I have clear visions and I start them one at a time.

·I am comfortable asking for help from other people.

·I like meeting new people.

The positive mindset is about to happen. You set your mind on the right things, the right way. This creates the momentum you need to get the results you want in your career, relationships, spiritual commitment, purpose, health, and wealth. It is ultimately up to you to set the course of how you want your life to work out. Your mind can be set to reach all these desires, but you must set your mind on being great. There are eight specific things you can do to set your mind on being great:

1. Speak Your Truth

What areas in your life are you strong at or excel in?
What areas in your life are you weak or need improvements?

You must first speak the truth about yourself to the world. Now mentally arrange the answers about your strong and weak points in your mind. These answers require honesty with yourself to get to the root of any problems, issues, or mental blocks you may have. **The Momentum of Success Technique** requires that your mind be consumed with only having positive thoughts traveling through it.

Your new norm is to have a daily routine of consciously thinking freely. Afterwards, verbalize your thoughts to yourself and the world. Complex thoughts are simply thinking of ways to become successful in all areas of your life. You're simplifying your thinking and the depth of your mind is set on directing your next move and protecting your gifts. Any complex thoughts can be divided into smaller simple thoughts to discover the truth inside of what you think and speak. Finally, what you think and speak correspond with your results.

2. Absolute Belief

Do you believe in your talents?
Do you have the confidence to start your own business?

JUST BELIEVE! The opinions of others have little merit on your purpose. There are fascinating ideas of purpose wandering through your mind because you have a philosophy of absolute belief. Be committed to communicate clear expectations of your desires. You hope to go back to school. You hope to be healthy.

You hope that all your credit cards are paid off. You hope to be used by GOD. You hope to be great at your job. You hope to have the courage to start your own business now. Express all your HOPES with the premise that they are obtainable. You must absolutely **believe** that you can and will succeed.

The habit of hope is what you possess. It increases your confidence level to believe in yourself. Your internal voice matches your interpretation from the bible. Therefore, you only trust what the word of God says about you. The Habit of Hope encourages you to keep your promise to fulfill your purpose. With absolute belief your expectations are to aim higher and put forth more effort. Now your hope is delivered with an intentional habit of ABSOLUTE BELIEF.

Your Greatest Expectations Meet Your Durable Determination.

The instant you have Absolute Belief, you expect all your goals to be achieved. You are full of BS!!! This BS I am writing about is your BELIEF SYSTEMS. It is important to have the right point of view of yourself. How do you truly see yourself? What is your opinion about your physical appearance? Do you sometimes judge your worth based on what is in your bank account?

Things change when beliefs change. Speak your truth and absolutely believe, then you will be engulfed with **The Momentum of Success Technique**. You just created another set of eyes that show who you are: worthy of the double salary promotion, motivated to exercise and eat healthy, approved for a small business loan, enjoying your life to the fullest, and consistently spending quality time with family.

Always thoroughly investigate your belief systems to make sure you resolve any doubts, fears, convictions, or feelings of being ashamed. The solution for your success in any area of your life is to have expectations that push you to excel and the determination to never stop believing in yourself. Protect your mindset to accomplish the most from your belief systems. Only have creative, positive, and inspiring things to enter your mind to maintain your absolute belief. As a result, there is a confidence generator flowing with absolute belief inside of you concerning your abilities and skills. After absolute belief, your focus has to be on the Positive.

3. Focus on Positive

Concentrate! Concentrate! Concentrate! You have the ability to direct the focus of your thoughts. Pay close attention to what thoughts enter your mind. Imagine you have the ability to put all of your views, suggestions, ideas, desires, and dreams under a microscope. Take inventory of your thoughts for seven days. Get a sheet a paper out and draw a line in the middle. On the top left write Positive and on the top right write Negative. After seven days total your list of thoughts. Do you focus more on the positive or negative? This world is full of negative energy that has an influence on what people focus on. Understand in your mind there is a brainstorm of hopes, fears, wants, doubts, goals, dreams, confidence, etc. Based on your environment, the components of this brainstorm are fighting for a position in your mind. Your daily fight is to focus on the positive. With concentration, you can see all things about you. The objective of the assignment is for you to get a self-guided tour of your mind and find your true positive focus.

You become everything you think. The results in your life are based on what you think. For the results to change, your thoughts must change. Therefore your negative thoughts can be redirected or replaced with positive thoughts. Positive Thoughts = Positive Results in your life. Intentionally set your thoughts on the positive position. In this life journey, you position yourself for success when you demand your thoughts to be positive about everything. Literally, make it an obsession to emphasize POSITIVITY. Only highlight happy, hopeful, exciting, thankful, and grateful components of your thoughts. To determine the destination in your life, start with the gears shifting to positive thinking at all cost. Positive energy is the guide to improve potential and approach purpose.

4. Visualize To Realize

Next, you must work visualization and connect it to everything you have in your imagination. Visualize every move that you are about to make. How can you start on your purpose and work a full-time job? When are you going to pick up your dream? Dreams are what your mind must be filled with. Everyday inside your mind are dreams and goals. Close your eyes and let your imagination draw the picture perfect life that you desire. Color these mental pictures by being exact and accurate to the penny, name, date, time, amount, etc. This visualization is your great masterpiece. You're the director for the mental pictures in your mind. Customize your mental pictures to pinpoint the growth of potential and the methods you will take to reach your purpose. *Your mind has the power and authority to visualize your success before your actual eyes can. The road map for success is created in the trenches of your mind.*

5. Stretch Your Mind

Even though the human brain only weighs about 3 pounds, it is a very important adaptive muscle that is used daily. In **The M.O.S.T.,** you exercise or stretch your mind. The muscle memory of success has great potential when you are constantly reading and seeking training. *The greatest muscle is to exercise your mind, and stretch your mind by reading books and doing training.* Study all information concerning your field of expertise. Learn from the best to be the best. Read books, watch videos, attend seminars, and take classes.

6. Unfold Your Dream

Dreams are never meant to be on a shelf collecting dust. Your dreams are meant to be unfolded for the original purpose to help people. The greatest possibility of achievement for your dreams is to be in the unfolded state. Your mind concentrates on your dream. Put your heart into things you desire. Actions to accomplish your dream are filled with passion. Now is the time to unfold your dream to the world. Your mind is set on the right things. Focus on your dreams. The greatest companions for your dreams are discipline and determination. Your dream is to be on display for the world to see and experience. *God has given you specific talents and gifts that help enhance your dream.* Your dream is tailored-made to fit the qualities you were born with. A perfect match. People are waiting for you to share your dream with them. Have a new Grand Opening to re-launch your dreams. Unfold your dreams now. *Hold the image of your dreams in the center of your mind.* Make your dreams stick this time. Work on your dreams daily. It is in you, it is inside you, and it is about you. You can achieve your dreams today.

· Unfold your dream of opening a restaurant.
· Unfold your dream of becoming a realtor.
· Unfold your dream of losing weight.
· Unfold your dream of owning a non-profit business.
· Unfold your dream of being healed of an illness.
· Unfold your dream of earning a college degree.
· Unfold your dream of being debt free.
· Unfold your dream of getting married & having kids.
· Unfold your dream of financial independence.
· Unfold your dream of being a millionaire.

7. Concentrate On Being Great

Focus on solutions and never the problems. Then you will be Great. *Your concentration will give you the directions of how to renew your mind daily or empty your mind.* Then and only then can you tap into your born potential of becoming great at your job, career, or profession. Study other successful people to get new ideas. Use this as a tool of referencing the mindsets of other great people you admire, to assist you in discovering your central focus for improvement, advancement, and accomplishment. These mindsets can be learned, and you can practice them in daily life situations that come up. *The key to focusing on being Great is for you to treat it like a faithful mate to your destiny.* It is going to require trust, commitment, communication, and faithfulness at all times. Spend as much time as you can on thinking about being Great. Be faithful about having a mindset of being great. *Greatness follows great ideas.* What is your next Great Idea?

8. Meditate To Be Transformed

Meditation is a good tool to help set your mind on being great. Your success is a spiritual journey that requires meditation on the Word of God. Set the atmosphere for what you think. Whether at home or work, locate a quiet place without distractions. At a scheduled time every day as you are studying the word of God, relax your mind. Then your mind will be filled with spiritual guiding principles to assist you in strategically thinking of ways to fulfill your dreams and goals. God has created you not to be a typical thinking person. However, an optimistic thinker's main desire is to accomplish the original purpose that God has for you. Please, include breaks during your meditation for transforming your mind to prepare for the great things ahead for you.

These eight things will set your mind on being Great. Now you can be creative, innovative, and motivated. Be inspired, dedicated, and determined. When you have your mind set on being Great, that positions you for promotion, advancement, and achievement. In a crowded room, you stand out because your mind is set on being great. People recognize your greatness and ask you for advice. You set your mind on being great and now you're ready for what life has to offer you. Even if you fall down, lose a job, or have a breakup in a relationship, you're able to bounce back because you have trained your mind to be resilient in times of turmoil. No man, woman, child, or any event can move you off of the mindset of being Great. Your confidence is built up to an all time high. Go for it all and continue to pursue your goals and your dreams. Strive for it, believe it, achieve it, and receive it. It is done, it is complete, your mind is set on being great and you are great!

25 Powerful Ways to Think Greater
Breakthrough Behaviors & Beliefs

1. Create habits of success.
2. Develop methods of monitoring yourself.
3. Every day make little steps to completing your goals.
4. Collect all the helpful data you need.
5. Use your cell phone as a tool to record mental notes.
6. Read books to expand your philosophy of success.
7. Always make your to-do-list a day in advance.
8. Categorize your list of things, complete by level of importance.
9. Always complete the most difficult task first.
10. Improve your decision making skills.
11. Make decisions as though the money is in the bank.
12. Keep organized mental notes of personal, business, and spiritual activities.
13. Investigate more than one scenario for each decision.
14. Only consider the best case scenarios.
15. In the forefront of your mind, all goals are achievable.
16. Trust your first instinct and make moves with precision.
17. The success found in failure is that you learned a lesson.
18. Remove negative thoughts from your mind.
19. Be honest with yourself to discover your strengths and weaknesses completely.
20. Encourage feedback, criticism, or advice from supporters.
21. Be able to positively process both good and bad feedback.
22. Make consistent corrections until you reach your goal.
23. Cultivate your gifts, talents, and skills with personal development.
24. Mainly focus on getting dynamic results.
25. Develop a solid plan to succeed.

Do you want to accomplish your career, business, family, and relationship goals faster?

Apply the 25 techniques for 21 days to create powerful success habits. Now your mind is in the center of the **Momentum of Success** and everything you touch shall prosper. Your daily routine is "success" when you use these principles.

10 Questions To Develop A Great Mindset

1. What can you do to maintain a positive mindset and stay in control of your destiny?

_____

_____

2. What strategic plan can you create to accomplish success?

_____

_____

3. What can help you to totally believe in yourself and your abilities to achieve your goals?

_____

_____

_____

4. What risks must you take to experience your full potential daily?

_____

_____

10 Questions To Develop A Great Mindset (cont'd.)

5. What knowledge can you gain from your coworkers, competitors, or family?

_____

_____

6. How can you challenge the greatness inside of you to come out?

_____

_____

7. What inspires you the most about successful people?

_____

_____

8. What do you embrace when you have setbacks or failures?

_____

_____

9. What is your path to master your gifts and talents?

_____

_____

10. What verbal feedback motivates you to stay focused?

_____

_____

Affirmation Instructions:

Write- Record Daily Affirmations on 3 pieces of paper or index cards (Place at home, car, and work)

State- Speak with a powerful tone and total belief 3 times a day: Morning, Evening, and Before bed.

Meditate- Think about affirmations at least 8 times (exercising, walking, driving, eating, working, etc.).

*14 interactions of the Daily Affirmations = a person's average of 450,000 daily thoughts.

Mindset
Affirmations

Monday

The momentum of success starts in my mind.
My mind starts my momentum of success.
The start of my momentum of success is in my mind.

Affirmation Instructions:

Write- Record Daily Affirmations on *3* pieces of paper or index cards (Place at home, car, and work)

State- Speak with a powerful tone and total belief *3* times a day: Morning, Evening, and Before bed.

Meditate- Think about affirmations at least *8* times (exercising, walking, driving, eating, working, etc.).

*14 interactions of the Daily Affirmations = a person's average of 450,000 daily thoughts.

Mindset Affirmations

Tuesday

My business is to think positive.
To think positive is my business.
I am in the business of thinking positive.

Affirmation Instructions:

Write- Record Daily Affirmations on 3 pieces of paper or index cards (Place at home, car, and work)

State- Speak with a powerful tone and total belief 3 times a day: Morning, Evening, and Before bed.

Meditate- Think about affirmations at least 8 times (exercising, walking, driving, eating, working, etc.).

*14 interactions of the Daily Affirmations = a person's average of 450,000 daily thoughts.

Mindset Affirmations

Wednesday

I renew my mind and supercharge my destiny.
I supercharge my destiny by renewing my mind.
My destiny supercharges when I renew my mind.

Affirmation Instructions:
Write- Record Daily Affirmations on 3 pieces of paper or index cards (Place at home, car, and work)
State- Speak with a powerful tone and total belief 3 times a day: Morning, Evening, and Before bed.
Meditate- Think about affirmations at least 8 times (exercising, walking, driving, eating, working, etc.).
*14 interactions of the Daily Affirmations = a person's average of 450,000 daily thoughts.

Mindset Affirmations

Thursday

My belief systems protect my dreams.
The protection of my dreams is my belief system.
My dreams are protected by my belief systems.

Affirmation Instructions:

Write- Record Daily Affirmations on 3 pieces of paper or index cards (Place at home, car, and work)

State- Speak with a powerful tone and total belief 3 times a day: Morning, Evening, and Before bed.

Meditate- Think about affirmations at least 8 times (exercising, walking, driving, eating, working, etc.).

*14 interactions of the Daily Affirmations = a person's average of 450,000 daily thoughts.

Mindset Affirmations

Friday

The eye for my vision is my mind.
My mind is the eyes for my vision.
I can see my vision through my mind.

Affirmation Instructions:

Write- Record Daily Affirmations on 3 pieces of paper or index cards (Place at home, car, and work)

State- Speak with a powerful tone and total belief 3 times a day: Morning, Evening, and Before bed.

Meditate- Think about affirmations at least 8 times (exercising, walking, driving, eating, working, etc.).

*14 interactions of the Daily Affirmations = a person's average of 450,000 daily thoughts.

<u>Mindset Affirmations</u>

Saturday

My mind is set on Massive Greatness.
Massive Greatness is my mindset.
I set my mind on Massive Greatness.

Affirmation Instructions:

Write- Record Daily Affirmations on *3* pieces of paper or index cards (Place at home, car, and work)

State- Speak with a powerful tone and total belief *3* times a day: Morning, Evening, and Before bed.

Meditate- Think about affirmations at least *8* times (exercising, walking, driving, eating, working, etc.).

*14 interactions of the Daily Affirmations = a person's average of 450,000 daily thoughts.

<u>Mindset Affirmations</u>

Sunday

I command my mind to make right decisions.
Right decisions are commanded by my mind.
My mind is commanded to make right decisions.

2. OPPORTUNITY

Jeremiah 29:11 (NIV) For I know the plans I have for you,"
declares the LORD, "plans to prosper you and not to harm you,
plans to give you hope and a future.

Possibilities In An Opportunity

Did you know that there is a greater chance of finding an opportunity rather than missing an opportunity? Life can be rough at times because you may lose a job or go financially bankrupt. Sometimes you can get an illness or sickness that limits your performance. I see the possibilities in an opportunity. You can too. We all have dreams. We all have goals. We all have desires. How do I start with the process of accomplishing my dreams? Do I focus on my current job or my ultimate dream? Because of trust issues most of us are afraid to connect with other people. Who will give me an opportunity? How do I find time to work on my dreams if I am so busy with work and family? Should I use some of my income to start my business? The answer to all the above questions is *"THERE ARE POSSIBILITIES IN OPPORTUNITIES."* Today, make the commitment to pursue your purpose. Tap into your great potential.

Where is your big opportunity?
What opportunity is present to embrace?
How can I pick the right opportunity?
When should I take advantage of an opportunity to start my business?
Will I ever have an opportunity to find my dream?

Opportunities are pieces of a puzzle that shape you as a Complete Masterpiece.

You just have to reach for an opportunity every day to materialize the ideal life that you have always dreamed of. *It is true that both dreams and fears are inside of an opportunity:*

·Your promotion is an opportunity.
·Your application for college is an opportunity.
·Your career is an opportunity.
·Your marriage is an opportunity.
·Your business is an opportunity.
·Your exercising is an opportunity.
·Your healthy eating is an opportunity.
·Your meeting new clients is an opportunity.
·Your moving to a different city is an opportunity.
·Your new position is an opportunity.
·Your church membership is an opportunity.
·Your serving in church is an opportunity.
·Your faith is an opportunity.

Your ideal life lies in an opportunity. The question is do you understand the possibilities in an opportunity? The opportunities exist around you everyday, this is a FACT. It is true; God has given you certain abilities that only you have possession of. I have always been the peacemaker and positive thinker. Currently, God has given me the opportunity to share my gift with the world.

There has to be a certain skill set to be able to take full advantage of every opportunity. As you are walking around in life like in a grocery store, you can grab a basket full of opportunities to move toward your goals. *The opportunity store is open 24 hours a day.* The opportunities are set to be the pathway to success. One opportunity transfers to another opportunity. Advance in life by being open to targeting different opportunities. The opportunity is a moment in time when there is prospect for great advancement. Take advantage of the opportune time when your job offers some free training that could otherwise cost a good amount of money. Do you attend the training? Today you have to invest in the various opportunities to reap the financial blessings associated with growth and promotion.

Start With A Mental Picture

I remember living the single life. Marriage never entered my mind, but everything changed in *ONE MOMENT*. That *ONE MOMENT* was an Opportunity. One day, I was at home in my alone time reflecting on my life and then it just happened. A Hunch….A Signal….. A Picture. In a soft voice I told myself, "I have all these Great Dreams and Big Goals but no one to share them with." Immediately afterwards, I had an opportunity to see a snapshot of my amazing future. Even though my future wife's face was blocked, I got a vivid mental picture of what it would be like to be happily married to my soulmate. I saw myself with my wife enjoying her company, sharing dreams, traveling the world, and raising our children together. WOW!!! This was a Mental Opportunity that changed my life forever! We have to be mindful that opportunities can be mental, physical, social, spiritual, or financial. This particular opportunity had the future components to change everything in my life.

IT WAS JUST THAT SERIOUS!!!

So this opportunity of a lifetime started with a thought. The next day, I went to my job and started speaking what I saw mentally. Verbally, I put into the atmosphere everything about my future marriage.

An Opportunity is the Greatest Confidence Builder of Your Future.

A typical day of working quietly at Publix was slicing meat for customers in the deli. At work I had laser focus only on helping my customers. After this mental opportunity, I started speaking more out loud at work. I confidently started saying, "My wife is coming, and she will be here in 30 days." Now, this was a very bold statement of faith with a date attached to it. *THIS IS AN OPPORTUNITY.* Overtaken with confidence, I got out of my comfort zone. As a deacon in church I was taught to declare and decree to God all the things I desire. The bold statements continued at work. Yes, customers and employees stared at me strangely, but I had no worries. What was important to me was to take advantage of this great opportunity. I happily walked around work shouting, "My wife is coming, and she will be here in 30 days!" Every day, I said this Opportunity Statement from six o'clock to eleven o'clock during my work shift at Publix. People were laughing at me and talking about me. Coworkers asked, "Shawn, where your wife at, where your wife at?" I confidently replied, "She is coming, she is coming, just believe me, she is coming!" I was consistent, persistent, and faithful in what I believed. This went on for weeks.

Even though, I had never met my soon to be wife, I made a conscious choice to visualize her in my mind. I had no clarity of her physical features but I knew how in love she made me feel. Each time I stated my affirmations, the visualization got clearer and stronger. I got in tune with my true hopes and desires. My work days got longer, but I kept speaking the things I wanted to experience:

One week went by and no new phone conversation.
Two weeks went by and no new friend.
Three weeks went by and no dates.
A month went by and no proposal.

From Disappointment To The Appointment

It was very disappointing and frustrating at times, but I knew there was an opportunity waiting just for me. You too have great opportunities waiting for you in spite of setbacks or failures. I had to continue to build a solid foundation of faith. The happy destination is to fulfill this opportunity. *AND THEN IT HAPPENED! Valery*, a former church member called and said, "God laid it on my heart to call you. Shawn, I want you to meet a young lady I know at my new church. I believe she is perfect for you." I replied, "Ok, but I don't do blind dates." I was only thinking about the risk of us not liking each other. I had to recognize that in an opportunity, there is always some doubt. In all rewards there are some levels of risks. So, I became open to making that one phone call. I made the phone call and to my surprise, it was a great conversation. We kept talking every day. We built a solid foundation of friendship from an opportunity. We became great friends before we started dating. I even brought my new girlfriend to Publix so coworkers and customers could meet my opportunity of happiness. What opportunity would make you happy? I proposed to her in six months, and we married in twelve months. It all started with a mental picture of an opportunity. Now, I am advancing every day in love, faith, happiness, and fulfilling my goals because of one opportunity.

An Opportunity Leads To Other Opportunities

Sometimes in life one opportunity is linked to another opportunity. The most important thing about an opportunity is you will know it is good for you when it is: *available, suitable, favorable, and valuable.* These are the four things you look for in an opportunity. (1) When an opportunity exists only for you it is available. It is yours for the taking. (2) The opportunity must be suitable. Worthy of your time and energy makes an opportunity correct for you. (3) It must be favorable, benefiting you and someone else. (4) Your opportunity must be valuable, which means yours skills and talents are worth a lot. This is when you take advantage of an opportunity. It must be available, suitable, favorable, and valuable. These are the four requirements to go find an opportunity every day.

Hidden Opportunities Are Around You

Opportunities are all around you every day. There are hidden opportunities surrounding you now. You have a dream, find an opportunity. You have a goal, find an opportunity. You have a desire, find an opportunity. Tap into the possibilities of an opportunity. It is for your advancement, development, and growth. Set the goals of achievement and accomplishment through discovering an opportunity. That is what an opportunity is for. The success you crave requires you to wisely use an opportunity. Take a chance to advance your career, marital status, or physical health. Immediately remove the risk factor and fear factor. Focus on having the faith factor in the opportunity. Just Believe! Go and get your opportunity. The opportunity for promotion, loving relationships, financial independence, and healing of a sickness is here. The opportunity for advancement is here. The opportunity for love is here. The opportunity for success is here. The opportunity for good health is here. Promote yourself to the next level today. Go find your opportunity now.

My Options Lead To My Purpose

In life you will always have options. Options are opportunities in disguise. In the most unlikely place, you can find an opportunity. Do something unconventional to discover the possible opportunity needed for dreams, desires, and purpose. Options are in your presence every day, but they often are overlooked for various reasons like fear of the unknown, low self esteem, pure doubt, or negative thinking. You better recognize that you have the right to use your options. God will always give you a way out of any situation. The better your relationship with God is, the more revelations you will have of the options that are available for you. The permission and right to utilize options is readily available for your purpose to be fulfilled.

I can recall working a part-time job for seven years from 6pm to 11pm nightly. For seven years, I felt stuck in a box. I was trapped inside a box of mediocrity because I was not operating in my purpose. I needed that extra money. Money was my personal need, but I was not walking in my purpose to teach children math. Worse of all, I was chasing pennies instead of purpose. A typical yearly raise was $.25-$.50 per hour. That is only about $260-$520 extra each year. The raises never were enough. I was working two jobs and still unhappy. For seven years, I felt as though I did not know what to do. I was stuck in place with no financial increase.

One day while at the part-time job, I started asking myself do I have any other options. Through studying the bible, it was revealed to me that I do have many options based on my faith in my purpose. Five years prior, a preacher prophesied to me that I would become a great math teacher with a big heart for helping students who struggle with mathematics. God can use other people to help you see the great potential inside of you to accomplish your purpose. Even though, I was at a part time job that was totally unconnected to my purpose, I still was able to find options out of this situation. Within these options there are 3 key ingredients:

1. Preference - My preference is to be happy and at peace with where I work. Can I take advantage of every opportunity to fulfill my purpose at this job? NO!

2. Possibility - I have the capability to operate in my God given abilities. God has a great purpose for me. Was there a possibility that my gifts and talents were not being used at this job? YES!
3. Choice- I have the power and the right to choose to stay or leave my job. Was the job paying all my bills? NO! Was I happy? NO!

Never Compromise Purpose For Pay

I was compromising my purpose for pay. I had low pay and high potential. Did they match? NO. I had a Masters Degree while working part-time at a grocery store. That did not match. Never compromise your purpose for pay! You can select the course for your potential. The three options you have are preference, possibility, and choice. I decided to use all three of my options pertaining to leaving Publix. Job transitions can be difficult because you're leaving your comfort zone. You will miss your managers and coworkers. Nevertheless, I chose PURPOSE!

In unfamiliar places you can still find your purpose. I had just gotten married, and was living in a totally new city. I got on the phone and started calling school systems. My first interview was not good. They said I did not have enough experience. I was denied my purpose one time! The second interview went well, but they chose another teacher. I was denied my purpose twice! Doubt entered my mind about my purpose. I was hurting mentally. My wife kept pushing me to continue to pursue my purpose. The doubt became unbearable. My mental ability to dream was being destroyed by doubt. I was about to give up.

What I needed was some motivation. Motivation is the required prescription to remove all negative thoughts and add a boost of confidence during the difficult process of discovering purpose. I had wasted countless years working on jobs that had nothing to do with my purpose. *To smell success you have to breathe motivation.* An inflow of motivation renewed my confidence. *It took one aspiration to fulfill my dreams.*

On that third interview, I was full of faith and confidence in getting my desired result. I walked through the school's entrance. I scanned the entire lobby and classrooms. Then I zoomed in on my purpose, the students! I observed the teachers conducting class. I said to myself, "This is the day that I get my job." I walked upstairs to meet the founder of the private school. Before the founder could ask me one interview question, I began to declare and decree, "I see students wearing school uniforms, and every student with a laptop. All students will be academically successful in mathematics and science. God is about to send you faithful, committed, and trustworthy teachers that will help you with your vision." It brought tears to the founder's eyes. She said, "How do you know this if you have never worked here?" I said, "God gave it to me!"

This was not a typical interview. It was a divine conversation where two purposes met. The founder had her purpose, and I had my purpose. Sometimes to find your purpose, you may have to link up with someone else's purpose. In this interview, my options met my purpose and potential. When you find your purpose there is a great promotion. I decided to quit my part-time job to pursue my purpose full time. So, I am declaring and decreeing on this day, "Use your options for your purpose, use your options for your potential, and use your options for your promotion!" You can do this! You must do it! You have to do it! Use your options. You have the right to use your options. Within these options you have your preference, possibility, and choice. Options exist all the time. You are never stuck because you are free to use your options. Walk into your life purpose now. You can do it. Within your options you will tap into your purpose, potential, and promotion. Choose the right options today.

11 Activation Words for Mastering Opportunities

1. CLEAR- Clearly have an understanding of your goals that produce the ideal opportunity for your destiny.

2. READY- Empower your mind with proficiency and methods to readily know what to do with available opportunities.

3. AUTHENTIC- Always be your original self. Embrace your authenticity, beliefs, and values.

4. SPECIALIZATION- Be an expert at your particular specialized skill. Opportunities cling to experts.

5. EXPECTATIONS- To be the best, you must challenge yourself and expect that there are better opportunities especially made for you.

6. PATIENCE- Be calm, relaxed, and positive as you move patiently toward your goals.

7. NETWORK- Relate to people who can help by networking to improve and achieve your goals.

8. IMAGINE- Use your imagination to have advanced creativity before an opportunity exists.

9. DISCOVER- By looking in often overlooked positions, the opportunity is discovered.

10. PLAN- In planning your steps, list all the benefits within an opportunity.

11. ACTION- Now is the perfect time to take action on an opportunity.

The M.O.S.T. Possibilities In An Opportunity
(Unscramble the words)

desire   possibility   authentic   promotion

ready   advancement   appointment   purpose

mental picture   valuable   expectations   available

faith   breakthrough   suitable   favorable

specialization   hope   benefit   discover

1. hftai   -   _ a _ _ _
2. aelaublv   -   _ a _ _ _ _ l _
3. okrrbuhgthae   -   _ _ _ a k _ _ r _ _ _ _
4. efobralav   -   _ _ _ _ _ a _ l _
5. ntacele imprut   -   m _ _ _ _ _ _   _ i _ _ _ r e
6. vidoercs   -   _ _ s _ o _ _ _
7. ialaalvbe   -   a _ _ _ l _ _ _ _
8. encmvtnaead   -   a _ _ _ _ _ c _ _ e _ _
9. etlbisua   -   s _ _ _ _ b _ _
10. tpnrimooo   -   p _ _ _ _ _ i _ _
11. etnpoantipm   -   _ _ _ _ _ _ n _ m _ _ t
12. sisyioitblp   -   p _ _ _ i _ _ _ _ _ t _
13. aptsalioicinze -   _ p _ c _ _ _ _ _ _ _ t _ o _
14. ttchniaue   -   _ _ _ _ e _ t _ _
15. ettexaspcnio   -   e _ _ _ _ _ _ a _ _ _ _ s
16. peoh   -   _ o _ _
17. ebfitne   -   b _ _ _ f _ _
18. sreeid   -   d _ _ i _ _
19. dryea   -   r _ _ _ _
20. puopres   -   _ u _ p _ _ _

Affirmation Instructions:

Write- Record Daily Affirmations on 3 pieces of paper or index cards (Place at home, car, and work)

State- Speak with a powerful tone and total belief 3 times a day: Morning, Evening, and Before bed.

Meditate- Think about affirmations at least 8 times (exercising, walking, driving, eating, working, etc.).

*14 interactions of the Daily Affirmations = a person's average of 450,000 daily thoughts.

Opportunity

Affirmations

Monday

My belief in myself is the magnet for opportunities.

The magnet for opportunities is me believing in myself.

The belief in myself is an opportunity magnet.

Affirmation Instructions:

Write- Record Daily Affirmations on 3 pieces of paper or index cards (Place at home, car, and work)

State- Speak with a powerful tone and total belief 3 times a day: Morning, Evening, and Before bed.

Meditate- Think about affirmations at least 8 times (exercising, walking, driving, eating, working, etc.).

*14 interactions of the Daily Affirmations = a person's average of 450,000 daily thoughts.

<u>Opportunity</u> <u>Affirmations</u>

Tuesday

I pursue opportunities for
breakthrough possibilities.
Breakthrough possibilities are why I
pursue opportunities.
Opportunities are pursued for possible
breakthroughs.

Affirmation Instructions:

Write- Record Daily Affirmations on 3 pieces of paper or index cards (Place at home, car, and work)

State- Speak with a powerful tone and total belief 3 times a day: Morning, Evening, and Before bed.

Meditate- Think about affirmations at least 8 times (exercising, walking, driving, eating, working, etc.).

*14 interactions with the Daily Affirmations = a person's average of 450,000 daily thoughts.

Opportunity

Affirmations

Wednesday

Self-development opens the windows
of opportunity.
The windows of opportunities are open
because of self-development.
Open the windows of opportunities
with self-development.

Affirmation Instructions:

Write- Record Daily Affirmations on *3* pieces of paper or index cards (Place at home, car, and work)

State- Speak with a powerful tone and total belief *3* times a day: Morning, Evening, and Before bed.

Meditate- Think about affirmations at least *8* times (exercising, walking, driving, eating, working, etc.).

*14 interactions with the Daily Affirmations = a person's average of 450,000 daily thoughts.

<u>Opportunity Affirmations</u>

Thursday

My specialization can open up new opportunities.

I can open a new opportunity with my specialization.

As I specialize in something, a new opportunity opens.

<u>Opportunity</u>

<u>Affirmations</u>

Friday

My key actions unlock unlimited
opportunities.
Unlimited opportunities are unlocked
by my key actions.
The key to unlocked unlimited
opportunities is action.

Affirmation Instructions:

Write- Record Daily Affirmations on *3* pieces of paper or index cards (Place at home, car, and work)

State- Speak with a powerful tone and total belief *3* times a day: Morning, Evening, and Before bed.

Meditate- Think about affirmations at least *8* times (exercising, walking, driving, eating, working, etc.).

*14 interactions with the Daily Affirmations = a person's average of 450,000 daily thoughts.

<u>Opportunity</u>

<u>Affirmations</u>

Saturday

My highest expectation every day is to meet an opportunity.

Every day my highest expectation meets an opportunity.

Meeting an opportunity is my highest expectation every day.

Affirmation Instructions:

Write- Record Daily Affirmations on *3* pieces of paper or index cards (Place at home, car, and work)

State- Speak with a powerful tone and total belief *3* times a day: Morning, Evening, and Before bed.

Meditate- Think about affirmations at least *8* times (exercising, walking, driving, eating, working, etc.).

*14 interactions with the Daily Affirmations = a person's average of 450,000 daily thoughts.

Opportunity Affirmations

Sunday

It is clear to me that opportunities
are always near.
Clearly, I see opportunities are near me.
Opportunities are always near and
clear to me.

3. Motivation

<u>Philippians 4:13 (MSG)</u> Whatever I have, wherever I am, I can make it through anything in the One who makes me who I am.

Motivation Is Your Vehicle To Success

Motivation is the vehicle to your destiny. For over 10 years, I had a great FEAR of writing a book and speaking publicly. Because of this fear, I was never motivated to pursue my true purpose and passion. Every time I was about to make a move of faith into my purpose, fear paralyzed my inspiration. Rarely would I change jobs or date exclusively. I was uncomfortable with experiencing the unfamiliar. I did not want to get hurt or be disappointed. Fear had a hold on my mind and it would not let go. Before you can maximize motivation, you have to destroy all levels of fear. My best definition of *FEAR is the acronym Faith Erased Aspiration Revoked.* Do you have any fears that are holding you back? To choose motivation over fear you have to stop making excuses, destroy all doubt, feel your fear, and keep your dream alive.

Stop Making Excuses

I learned in college that an excuse is: A tool used by non-achievers to receive worthless monuments of nothing but less than nothing. Non-achievers are underperformers, underachievers, or mediocre people. A person who makes excuses is not an accurate description of your work or performance. You are a person of power, purpose, and passion. Your success in performance is based on being persistent and productive. Nonstop pursuit of happiness is your mission.

Excuses are like upside down stairs that never lead to success.

There is little success in your life when you continue to make excuses. It is imperative that you stop making excuses to get the motivation you need to succeed. Stop walking down the stairs of excuses:

Downward Stairs Of Excuses

Stop making excuses for not spending quality time with your family.

Stop making excuses for not saving 10% of your income.

Stop making excuses for not regularly attending church.

Stop making excuses for not getting a yearly physical.

Stop making excuses for not starting your business.

Stop making excuses for not finishing school.

Stop making excuses for not using a budget.

Stop making excuses for not exercising.

succeSS

Excuse My Excuses

You can grant yourself the status of being exempt from excuses. Every time you make an excuse you have to say forgive me (excuse me). Examples you can say: "Excuse me for being lazy." "Excuse me for procrastinating." "Excuse me for having doubt." "Excuse me for being negative." "Excuse me for being fearful." "Excuse me for not pursuing my purpose." Say forgive me (excuse me) to all your excuses so you can walk in your purpose, visualize your destiny, accept God's calling, map out your vision, and pursue all your dreams.

Now become who you have been called to be. There is greatness inside of you but excuses are holding you back. What are you going to do about your excuses? Every desire you have for your life is postponed because of excuses. Give yourself permission to walk in your passion. Give yourself permission for a promotion. Give yourself permission to be a full-time entrepreneur. Give yourself permission to purposely be everything that God has called you to be. Say EXCUSE ME to your excuses! Defeat your excuses today. The three things you can do to defeat excuses are:

1. <u>Be careful of your language.</u> There are two words that must be eliminated from your life forever. "But" and "Not" are two words you must eliminate from your language. Have you ever said, "I want to be debt free but I need more money?" This "but" is an excuse. To help reduce debt, have a budget and avoid using credit cards. Excuses have never helped a person become debt free.

2. <u>Be careful of who you listen to.</u> Stop listening to people who complain and are not trying to do anything with their life. Avoid hanging around people who have a lazy or slothful spirit. People that doubt their potential and are afraid to discover their purpose can not influence you. Just stop listening to negative people.

Remove yourself from these negative people and then you remove excuses. Excuses are unhealthy for your career, finances, or relationship. Because fear is contagious, doubt is contagious, and laziness is contagious. Excuses are contagious. And you don't want to be contaminated with excuses.

3. <u>Be open to learning.</u> Pick some books up. Read some books. Take some classes. Go back to school. You have to always be in pursuit of learning something new. Because the more your learn, the more excuses are eliminated from your life. You now have wisdom, knowledge, and understanding.

These few tips eliminate excuses. You have the tools you need to succeed. Stop making excuses. Speak the correct language, avoid the wrong people, and continue to learn new things. Lastly, grant yourself permission to prosper in your potential and purpose.

Destroy All Doubt

I can't stand doubt! I hate what doubt stands for. I hate how doubt affects people. Doubt is not your friend, it is your foe. I can't stand doubt! Because of doubt, I would never have gotten married. I had to destroy doubt. Because of doubt, I would never have started my clothing line Favor Gear. You have to destroy doubt. Doubt makes a person fearful of whom they are. Doubt paralyzes your purpose. Your positive energy is overtaken by the negative energy of doubt. Please do not entertain doubt as an idea or habit. Doubt must be destroyed immediately. Today is the day that you destroy all doubt.

8 Ingredients To Fully Destroy Doubt

1. **Write it down**. Write down on a sheet of paper all your doubts or fears. With all your strength and might, ball that sheet of paper up and throw it away.

2. **Speak the truth**. Truth that is altered is doubt. You must find the truth in all doubt.

3. **Speak in the affirmative**. Your language of choice is to speak affirmations. Only speak what you desire in life.

4. **Make your vision and your purpose bigger**. Enlarge the reasons why you pursue your purpose with motivation. Gain confidence in accomplishing your vision.

5. **Develop yourself**. Cultivate your skills and gifts with training. Be motivated to learn new ways to become a better you.

6. **Renew a positive mindset**. Clear your mind of all negative thinking. Only think about the positive.

7. **Celebrate**. Find celebration in all failures and successes.

8. **Pray.** Continue to pray in confidence. Thank God for all He has done for you, and will do for you.

These eight ingredients will destroy doubt forever. Write a goodbye letter to doubt. The truth is doubt never was supposed to be near your purpose and potential. Speak in the affirmative of what you desire. Don't let doubt destroy your desire. Know without a shadow of doubt who directly benefits from your vision and purpose. The better you become through training and personal development, the less you doubt yourself. Thinking on the positive removes doubt from your mind. Celebrate successes and failures, therefore you're immune to doubt. Pray in faith, not with doubt. What is walking in front of you is determination and destiny. A Great Mindset gives you the strength and power to not be weakened by doubt. Your strong faith is undeniable; you can operate in your purpose with maximum potential. Because doubt can't hold you back, dream big enough to reach all your goals. Motivation has destroyed the doubt in your life. The good life you desire is yours. You're great. You're awesome. You're unstoppable. The sky's the limit. You have unlimited favor in your life. You're blessed. You have assurance on today that you are successful. Walk in your purpose and potential!

Feel Your Fear

1. **F**aith in your purpose, potential, and performance
2. **E**motional stability to overcome any doubt
3. **E**xcited about the possibilities in all opportunities
4. **L**ove the challenge to be resilient and persistent

Feel your fear of <u>becoming an entrepreneur</u> and *do it anyway.*
Feel your fear of <u>getting married</u> and *do it anyway.*
Feel your fear of <u>retiring</u> and *do it anyway.*
Feel your fear of <u>changing careers</u> and *do it anyway.*
Feel your fear of <u>purchasing a new home</u> and *do it anyway.*
Feel your fear of <u>applying for a business loan</u> and *do it anyway.*
Feel your fear of <u>having total faith in GOD</u> and *do it anyway.*
Feel your fear of <u>investing in stocks, bonds, & 401K</u> and *do it anyway.*

Feel your fear of <u>dating again</u> and *do it anyway.*
Feel your fear of <u>having children</u> and *do it anyway.*
Feel your fear of <u>applying for a new job</u> and *do it anyway.*
Feel your fear of <u>seeking spiritual counseling</u> and *do it anyway.*
Feel your fear of <u>going to the doctor</u> and *do it anyway.*
Feel your fear of <u>having surgery</u> and *do it anyway.*
Feel your fear of <u>daily exercise</u> and *do it anyway.*
Feel your fear of <u>starting an online business</u> and *do it anyway.*
Feel your fear of <u>eating healthy food</u> and *do it anyway.*
Feel your fear of <u>writing a book</u> and *do it anyway.*
Feel your fear of <u>going back to college</u> and *do it anyway.*
Feel your fear of <u>applying for a business license</u> and *do it anyway.*
Feel your fear of <u>investing in real estate</u> and *do it anyway.*
Feel your fear of <u>finding a mentor</u> and *do it anyway.*
Feel your fear of <u>leading other people</u> and *do it anyway.*
Feel your fear of <u>public speaking to a large audience</u> and *do it anyway.*
Feel your fear of <u>dreaming big</u> and *do it anyway.*
Feel your fear of <u>becoming a deacon or minister</u> and *do it anyway.*
Feel your fear of <u>joining a new church</u> and *do it anyway.*

You can sense or anticipate fear is about to come, then you have the opportunity to feel your fear and do it anyway.

The only two things true about fear are: You Can Feel It and Overcome It Today!

Allow your imagination to freely search for ways to set goals, improve your talents, take calculated risks, and help other people.

Keep Your Dream A.L.I.V.E.

Keep your dream alive. You must keep your dream alive. There are five basic things to do in order to keep your dream alive:

> **A** - Absolutely believe in your dream. Take some type of action on your dream daily. Your dreams are the employer and you're the worker. Motivation gives you the energy to pursue your dreams with no days off or breaks.
> **L** - Lead your dreams. You're the leader of your dreams. The interpretation of your dreams navigates your next move toward your purpose and passion.
> **I** - Invest in your dream with time & money. Sacrifice is an investment with a return on it. Maybe today, tomorrow, or in the future, but you will see a return on your investment. Always find ways to improve your dream.
> **V** - Vocalize to visualize your dream. Be excited every day. Wake up having silent conversations with yourself about your dreams. Verbally communicate your dreams to trusted family, friends, and coworkers. The more you vocalize your dreams, the more you can visualize your dreams. Take 10 minutes a day to see your dream in your mind. Visualize you accomplishing your dream, the steps you will take, and who you will connect with. Use your vision in your mind to see the roadmap of success.
> **E** - Empower yourself to dream. You must empower yourself with knowledge and skills to improve on your abilities. Read and study people that are successful. Study videos to challenge yourself. Connect with people that made it happen. Push yourself. Find someone who will be accountable to you and make you work harder.

Keep your dream alive! It has to stay alive! You must keep it alive. You were born to do this. The skills that you have only you can do. The abilities that you have only you can do. You're the leader of your dream. The Guiding Principle for your Dream is your Belief System. Do you believe in your dream? You got to absolutely believe, you have to lead, you have to invest, you have to vocalize to visualize, and you must empower yourself. Strengthen your mind, strengthen your voice, go with the courage, take a risk, you can do it. Keep your dream alive.

FEAR is the Greatest killer of MOTIVATION. That is why you must keep your Dream Alive.

Motivated To Speak

My dream has been to become a motivational speaker for over 15 years. I had never spoken in front of an audience. I had never even made a video of myself talking. That was a terrifying act to me. One night at 3:00 a.m., I was surfing videos on YouTube. I saw a video of somebody I knew from my former church, Anointed Word Christian Ministries. It was Kendall Ficklin, and he was telling people to Grind day and night until you reach your purpose. The videos were very inspiring and motivating. I watched about six videos and I was getting so pumped up.

Next, I started watching Eric Thomas's videos and he spoke with so much power. Something was waking up inside me. Then I started watching some of Les Brown's videos, and I was fully awakened then. I mean these videos were stirring up my unfulfilled dream of becoming a motivational speaker. I always liked hearing Les Brown speak because he is a great story teller.

For years I wanted to be a motivational speaker but I had no motivation to start because of fear, doubt, and excuses.

I began to see myself speaking the way Kendall Ficklin, Eric Thomas, and Les Brown spoke in the videos. "Enough is Enough! Too many years have been wasted because of my low self confidence and fear of working for success," I said to myself. I had to try something different like getting a mentor. To me, a mentor is a person who has levels of success that I desire to accomplish and is willing to give me support and tools I need to be successful. Immediately, I thought about reaching out to Kendall Ficklin. Doubt said, "He will not remember you." Excuses said, "He is too busy traveling to take time and talk to you." Fear said, "You know that you're afraid to ask for help." Procrastination said, "Wait to next month to call him." Yes, I had a full-time job, but I still had my dream of being a motivational speaker. I set an appointment to talk to doubt, fear, excuses, and procrastination. I said to the things that were stopping me from achieving my dreams, "NO!" I picked the phone up, called Kendall and asked him to be my mentor. I joined his group called GRINDATION, which has over 100 people just like me. Kendall, my mentor said, "GRIND to get small wins every day, that lead to big wins, just trust me." I obeyed my mentor's commands to achieve my dreams, and I haven't stopped GRINDING to this day.

Now, motivation to fulfill my dreams was constant along with cultivating my gifts and talents. My destiny was to reach and motivate people, but I'd never recorded anything. On that night, I was so inspired that I made my first video. It was so exciting to see myself on a video. It boosted my confidence. Getting Kendall to be my mentor and this one act of confidence started me on a journey to fulfill my dream. Fear, doubt, and excuses are always on the road of success. Motivation alone can destroy being afraid, procrastinating, and hesitating to fulfill your dreams. To accomplish every goal, you need to apply these 4 helpful things and stay motivated:

Routines of Motivation

1. Daily meditation - This helps you concentrate on the needs for your life.
Keep a current list of your family's needs, spiritual desires, and purpose needs.

2. Reflection - Review past mistakes and successes to learn valuable lessons about futures moves.

3. Contemplation - Carefully consider the pros and cons of each decision. Destiny is depending on you to make the right decisions.

4. Inspiration - That is the product of creative thinking and work. Look deep inside yourself to find out what you actually want to accomplish. How will you achieve every goal? How do you feel about reaching your goals?

Destiny is your portion.
Destiny is your path.
Destiny is your assignment.
Destiny is your target.
Destiny is reached through motivation.

Motivation is your vehicle to your destiny. When you reach your destiny, you experience accomplishing your ultimate goal, using your strongest skills, achieving your economic desire, finding your primary focus, believing your religious perspective, activating your dominant thought, and pursuing success patiently. Motivation is your vehicle to your destiny. Motivation pushes you into your purpose. Motivation propels your potential to be great. Motivation helps you achieve your goals. Your destiny is near. Your destiny is here. Walk in your purpose to accomplish your dreams with motivation.

Motivation Statements

1. You can have a motivating life when you meditate and concentrate on these things: _____
_____.

2. What inspires you? Who inspires you? Why?_____
_____

3. How can you achieve your goals?_____
_____.

4. What effort can you use to motivate yourself to accomplish your goals?_____
_____.

5. My motivation is to be the best_____
so I can_____my_____.

Affirmation Instructions:

Write- Record Daily Affirmations on *3* pieces of paper or index cards (Place at home, car, and work)

State- Speak with a powerful tone and total belief *3* times a day: Morning, Evening, and Before bed.

Meditate- Think about affirmations at least *8* times (exercising, walking, driving, eating, working, etc.).

*14 interactions with the Daily Affirmations = a person's average of 450,000 daily thoughts.

Motivation

Affirmations

Monday

I am motivated to be my best "me".

To be my best, I motivate myself.

Staying motivated gets the best

out of me.

Affirmation Instructions

Write- Record Daily Affirmations on 3 pieces of paper or index cards (Place at home, car, and work)

State- Speak with a powerful tone and total belief 3 times a day: Morning, Evening, and Before bed.

Meditate- Think about affirmations at least 8 times (exercising, walking, driving, eating, working, etc.).

*14 interactions with the Daily Affirmations = a person's average of 450,000 daily thoughts.

Motivation

Affirmations

Tuesday

What motivates me more than anything is my "why".
My "why" motivates me more than anything.
More than anything, my "why' motivates me.

Affirmation Instructions:

Write- Record Daily Affirmations on *3* pieces of paper or index cards (Place at home, car, and work)

State- Speak with a powerful tone and total belief *3* times a day: Morning, Evening, and Before bed.

Meditate- Think about affirmations at least *8* times (exercising, walking, driving, eating, working, etc.).

*14 interactions with the Daily Affirmations = a person's average of 450,000 daily thoughts.

Motivation

Affirmations

Wednesday

My inspiration comes from quality time with my family.

Quality time with my family is my inspiration.

The quality of my family time inspires me.

Affirmation Instructions:

Write- Record Daily Affirmations on *3* pieces of paper or index cards (Place at home, car, and work)

State- Speak with a powerful tone and total belief *3* times a day: Morning, Evening, and Before bed.

Meditate- Think about affirmations at least *8* times (exercising, walking, driving, eating, working, etc.).

*14 interactions with the Daily Affirmations = a person's average of 450,000 daily thoughts.

Motivation

Affirmations

Thursday

Big goals are achieved with small wins.

Small wins achieve big goals.

Achieve big goals with small wins.

Affirmation Instructions:

Write- Record Daily Affirmations on *3* pieces of paper or index cards (Place at home, car, and work)

State- Speak with a powerful tone and total belief *3* times a day: Morning, Evening, and Before bed.

Meditate- Think about affirmations at least *8* times (exercising, walking, driving, eating, working, etc.).

*14 interactions with the Daily Affirmations = a person's average of 450,000 daily thoughts.

Motivation

Affirmations

Friday

I am capable of being able to complete my task.

I complete my task because I am capable and able.

My task is complete because I am able and capable.

Affirmation Instructions:

Write- Record Daily Affirmations on *3* pieces of paper or index cards (Place at home, car, and work)

State- Speak with a powerful tone and total belief *3* times a day: Morning, Evening, and Before bed.

Meditate- Think about affirmations at least *8* times (exercising, walking, driving, eating, working, etc.).

*14 interactions with the Daily Affirmations = a person's average of 450,000 daily thoughts.

Motivation

Affirmations

Saturday

I have the meaningful goal of
being successful.
Being successful is my meaningful goal.
I am meant to be successful.

Affirmation Instructions:

Write- Record Daily Affirmations on *3* pieces of paper or index cards (Place at home, car, and work)

State- Speak with a powerful tone and total belief *3* times a day: Morning, Evening, and Before bed.

Meditate- Think about affirmations at least *8* times (exercising, walking, driving, eating, working, etc.).

*14 interactions with the Daily Affirmations = a person's average of 450,000 daily thoughts.

Motivation

Affirmations

Sunday

I create a motivating climate
to do everything.
Everything I do creates a
motivating climate.
My climate motivates me to be creative.

4. Enthusiasm

1 Thessalonians 5:16-18 ESV. Rejoice always, pray
without ceasing, and give thanks in all
circumstances; for this is the will of God in Christ
Jesus for you.

Enthusiasm Is Your Greatest Asset

Your enthusiasm is your greatest asset. The energy you have is a direct force for promotion and wealth to approach you. For those seeking a job or already have job, my greatest advice is to study successful managers, businessmen, or entrepreneurs. Get maximum equity in your company by adding the value of enthusiasm in your work effort. I can recall during the process of every promotion in my life, I would have meetings with specific managers, who all would express the same one thing that made me different. All the managers said, "Your enthusiasm is your greatest asset."

Enthusiasm S.W.A.G.G.

I learned all there is to know about enthusiasm from a former Publix deli manager, his name was Mike. Mike was a Caucasian young guy about 24 years old, brown hair a little spiked, and he loved playing the guitar. He was my assistant manager in the deli at Publix store #1183 with an all African American staff. But Mike had **S.W.A.G.G.: Supportive of staff, Willing to learn, Always enthusiastic, Giving to others, and Great at his job**. Mike was known by all staff for leaving lengthy "to do" lists for each employee. This often rubbed the employees the wrong way. I rarely worked with Mike because of my shift, but Pat's (the deli manager) daughter was about to graduate so she had to switch schedules with Mike for a short period of time. The first day of closing with Mike, we had a major disagreement about how to close meat slicers in our traditional work station. So I was upset, but I did what Mike told me to do and it worked out perfectly. Actually, with Mike we closed and finished cleaning the deli earlier than normal. Mike talked fast, walked fast, worked fast, and gave orders fast. That fast pace of working intrigued me and inspired me to perform better. I had to find out how Mike became so successful at such a young age.

Make History With Enthusiasm

I sat down with Mike one day and to my amazement I learned one of the most valuable lessons from a person that was twice as young as me. *Being fueled with enthusiasm speeds up your success and increases your potential.* Through conversation, I learned that Mike was promoted to assistant deli manager because he kept pushing toward his goals, in spite of the good and bad things happening. Mike was one of the youngest employees promoted to management at store #1183 because of his work ethic, enthusiasm, and consistent performance.

Interview About Enthusiasm

My first question I asked Mike was, "Why did they pick such a young person like you as a candidate for management?" Mike said, "I guess they believed I would be a great manager because my maturity in the areas of working with so much passion. I have a personality that genuinely loves learning new things. These two things helped them with their decision." Mike mentioned to me that when he was working part-time at Publix that his car had broken down, and he didn't have enough money to get it repaired. Mike said, "In this time of desperation, I had to find some determination." Mike was so determined that he walked almost 3 miles whether rain, sleet, snow, or sunny to get to work. He had difficulties and struggles, but he maintained his enthusiasm to work. This enthusiasm did not go unnoticed. Whenever Mike worked overtime, Pat and other managers always took time to give him advice and tips on success. Mike had such a ridiculous hunger for learning that he passed the Manager's test on his first try. Mike was promoted to assistant deli manager at Publix through perseverance, determination, and enthusiasm. Through conversation and observation with Mike, I learned fourteen valuable attributes of enthusiasm that made him great and can make you great too.

14 Attributes of Amazing Enthusiasm

Happiness

The quickest and easiest way to be full of enthusiasm is for you to BE HAPPY. Routinely be happy. Make a list of everything that makes you happy. Include hobbies, stress relievers, relaxing moments, events, etc. Sometimes refer to the "happy list" to keep you excited about life. Give yourself unlimited permission to have the Happiness Habit. Do things you like, watch things that excite you, eat things that are delicious to you, and travel to places you enjoy. What you like makes you happy. Being happy leads to recharging your enthusiasm for accomplishing your goals.

Goal Oriented

Have a Plan to have a Plan to Plan your Purpose Plan.
Enthusiasm skyrockets during the planning phase, whether it is your promotion, purpose, or performance. Make sure to write down your most important ideas. This plan gives you a map of how to define, measure, and execute the steps needed to move toward your goals. As you are planning, you start to see yourself achieving all your goals. Afterwards, the action that follows your plan is effortless, exciting, and energized.

Setting goals is a motivating tool you need to form enthusiasm in your everyday life.

Organized

Whenever you are unorganized, you can deflate your wheels of enthusiasm. The key components for your success must be organized like a crystal clear mind, goal made of concrete, and an immaculate work area. Everything that relates to your potential and purpose must be in the right order to get effective results. You have organized systems that keep you focused on finishing what you start. This increases your enthusiasm because you have maximum productivity in your thoughts, desires, and performance.

Think outside the box filled with change, for a chance.

Creative

Let your thoughts be free to explore the unknown and unfamiliar. When you have enthusiasm, you are inspiring your imagination to be a creative master of your fate. Creativity provokes you to stay enthusiastic about your desires. Create something that has never been done before. Use the full capacity of your innovation and imagination in a spontaneous manner to produce a concrete plan to reach all your dreams. Raise the bar on your enthusiasm for a high level of life. Challenge yourself to face the difficult obstacles with ease. Find new and improved ways of solving problems better than before. Get excited about creating a bright future!

Proactive

When you are the creator of something new, you become the "go to" person for action. Monumental enthusiasm is produced when you're positive, proactive, and purposeful in your efforts to complete things that you value the most. Be that "go to" person who gets things done quickly. Be so excited about your purpose that you have passion to take advance action on your dreams, goals, and desires. Finally, have the greatest view of your dreams by working in front of them. Realize you can accomplish your desires faster with enthusiasm.

Patient

Be honest, is God patient with you? Yes of course! Impatience is a fast way to damage enthusiasm permanently. Know that God is in control, you must be more patient for success to happen. Be patient even if the process takes a long time or you will get off course. Impatience leads to frustration; that is why you abort traveling down that road. A lifetime of enthusiasm is experienced through you being able to afford the valuable price of having patience in everything you do. With patience, you're in control to set the pace at which you reach success.

Positive

Seek to find something good in everything. Being positive keeps your enthusiasm alive. Even when things may go bad, let that inspire you to keep pursuing your dreams. Be excited about life and draw strength every time you have success or failure. Be sure to have the Positive Energy of Enthusiasm.

Passionate

To build the unshakable enthusiasm, you must have electrifying passion by operating in your full potential. As the morning sun rises, get out of your bed to become the best you today. You're pumped up and excited about what life has to offer you. Your passion ignites perseverance in you that can withstand any great fall or setback. *Love what you do and who you are, then enthusiasm is constant in your life.*

Gratitude

First of all, you have to be grateful to be alive. There are unlimited opportunities to become what you were created to be. Whether little or large accomplishments, be grateful for all things. Grind of Life sometimes seems unfair, but all things will work together for your good. Be grateful. Make a list of things you are grateful for: God, spouse, parents, kids, family, job, health, right mindset, knowledge, achievements, relationships, etc. You have the potential to have so much enthusiasm by having gratitude.

Life is easier and you perform at your best when you're grateful and thankful.

Prideful

Always be proud of who you are, where you came from, and your future prospects. *A stepping stone for enthusiasm is you having the convincing confidence in your greatness potential.* Sometimes you need a confidence boost from your spouse, family, friends, or coworkers. *A carry-on bag to success is full of pride for the work you have done.* Your pride impacts your work and in return you are excited about working. Know who you are becoming so people can understand who you are too.

Reasonable

Respect your potential and have reasonable expectations of your skills and knowledge. Put yourself in situations where your true potential is realized. Never exaggerate your worth. *Potential greatness is yours because you were born to solve problems, invent new things, and help people.* Your excitement for helping other people is your reasonable service. Stay excited and reasonable about all your future endeavors, whether good or bad.

Inspirational

Believe in yourself no matter what happened, occurs, or will exist. You have to inspire yourself when no one else will. You're inspired to move toward life with enthusiasm. Show that you are committed to your goals by pursuing them with joy, happiness, and confidence. Inspiration has the power to pick up enthusiasm on every occasion.

Improvement

Your full potential is realized the moment you dwell in self improvement. As you grow in relationships, careers, health, and wealth you gain more enthusiasm than anticipated. All people become enthusiastic about personal and professional development. Your life gets better and greater because you accept the reality that you must experience improvement daily in order for success to happen. Happily push growth and development. People of various backgrounds are looking at your growth as a testament for their desire to improve their current situation. Recognize that life is all about using situations as a measuring tool for a constant means of growth. The steps you make toward achievement require your focus. The reward for improvement is the enthusiasm to have a purposeful life.

Enthusiastic People

You become the company you hang with. People who are negative, doubtful, or fearful can contaminate your chance of being great. Avoid these people at all cost. Also, enthusiasm is really contagious. It is the group of enthusiastic people who you should desire to hang around. Be bound for greatness. Even at your lowest points in life, the enthusiastic group of friends will help you to feed off the energy that great things are about to happen. On the flipside, get rid of negative people that zap away your energy. Associate with people who have balance between inspiration and motivation. This is the boost you need to achieve your goals, dreams, and potential.

These fourteen vital things make your enthusiasm the greatest asset for any employer or new job. Your goal is to always aim to win with the great asset of enthusiasm. Organize your motivation to know the starting and ending points of achieving your goals. Creativity gives you an arsenal of innovative ways to get things done. To be proactive means you have strategically planned for massive productivity in everything that you do. Be patient by relaxing and meditating. Have a can do positive attitude at all times. Offer random acts of kindness daily. Your enthusiasm is your greatest asset. Therefore, promotion is here. Therefore, a new job responsibility is here. Therefore, increase in income is here. It is done and it is done. Your enthusiasm is your greatest asset because you're a motivated learner, dedicated worker, and you have a passion for action. Because you have enthusiasm, positive people are drawn to you. You're a leader by nature. Your enthusiasm is your power to propel you into purpose. Your enthusiasm opens doors for success. Your enthusiasm can lead people by example. Dedicate yourself to enthusiasm because it is your greatest asset.

Follow the fourteen strategies described above in order to kindle the fire of enthusiasm and keep it burning until you've achieved everything that you want. If you think of each of your goals as a seed that you're planting, enthusiasm is the fertilizer that helps the seed to grow.

Your Enthusiasm Checklist

Check your inventory of enthusiasm daily.

__ Smiling   __Compliment Others

__Friendly to People   ___Positive

__Organized Workstation   __Random Act of Kindness

__Practice Patience   __Help Others

__Respectful   __Prideful

___Grateful   __Understanding

__Hopeful Habit   __Consistent Effort

___Small Wins   __Dream Big

___Family Time   __Conquer Fear

___Determination   __Seeking Knowledge

___Priority List   __Worked on Goals

___Forgave Someone   __Supported Someone Else

Tap Into Your Enthusiasm

Maintain your enthusiasm despite setbacks or failures.

1. List things I must stop worrying about. _____

_____

2. What is my task at work that I give total commitment and maximum energy to?_____

_____

3. How can I eliminate procrastination of my goals and dreams?_____

_____

4. List 3 people I can trust with information concerning my marriage, job, goals, business, faith._____

_____

5. The top goals I must concentrate on daily are:

_____

6. The next moves, changes, and transitions I can focus on are: _____

_____

7. My reasons why I enjoy my job, marriage, school, my business, etc. are:

_____

8. The reasons I take pleasure in dreaming, setting goals, and planning are:

_____

_____

Affirmation Instructions:

Write- Record Daily Affirmations on 3 pieces of paper or index cards (Place at home, car, and work)

State- Speak with a powerful tone and total belief 3 times a day: Morning, Evening, and Before bed.

Meditate- Think about affirmations at least 8 times (exercising, walking, driving, eating, working, etc.).

*14 interactions with the Daily Affirmations = a person's average of 450,000 daily thoughts.

Enthusiasm

Affirmations

Monday

Passion and excitement require
immediate action.
Immediate action requires
passion and excitement.
My passion requirements are
excitement and immediate action.

Affirmation Instructions:

Write- Record Daily Affirmations on 3 pieces of paper or index cards (Place at home, car, and work)

State- Speak with a powerful tone and total belief 3 times a day: Morning, Evening, and Before bed.

Meditate- Think about affirmations at least 8 times (exercising, walking, driving, eating, working, etc.).

*14 interactions with the Daily Affirmations = a person's average of 450,000 daily thoughts.

Enthusiasm

Affirmations

Tuesday

My enthusiasm is the force that clears
my purpose path.

The clear path of purpose happens
with enthusiasm.

The path to my purpose is cleared
with enthusiasm.

Affirmation Instructions:

Write- Record Daily Affirmations on 3 pieces of paper or index cards (Place at home, car, and work)

State- Speak with a powerful tone and total belief 3 times a day: Morning, Evening, and Before bed.

Meditate- Think about affirmations at least 8 times (exercising, walking, driving, eating, working, etc.).

*14 interactions with the Daily Affirmations = a person's average of 450,000 daily thoughts.

<u>Enthusiasm</u>
<u>Affirmations</u>

Wednesday

I am so eager to learn new skills and concepts.

My concept is to always be eager to learn a new skill.

Be open to working on a new concept to get new skills.

Affirmation Instructions:

Write- Record Daily Affirmations on 3 pieces of paper or index cards (Place at home, car, and work)

State- Speak with a powerful tone and total belief 3 times a day: Morning, Evening, and Before bed.

Meditate- Think about affirmations at least 8 times (exercising, walking, driving, eating, working, etc.).

*14 interactions with the Daily Affirmations = a person's average of 450,000 daily thoughts.

Enthusiasm

Affirmations

Thursday

I am wholeheartedly committed to pursuing my goals.

I commit to pursue my goals with my whole heart.

My heart is committed to pursuing my goals.

Affirmation Instructions:

Write- Record Daily Affirmations on 3 pieces of paper or index cards (Place at home, car, and work)

State- Speak with a powerful tone and total belief 3 times a day: Morning, Evening, and Before bed.

Meditate- Think about affirmations at least 8 times (exercising, walking, driving, eating, working, etc.).

*14 interactions with the Daily Affirmations = a person's average of 450,000 daily thoughts.

Enthusiasm

Affirmations

Friday

My surroundings have positive people
that empower and energize me.
I am empowered and energized by
being around positive people.
Associating with positive people makes
me feel empowered and energized.

Affirmation Instructions:

Write- Record Daily Affirmations on 3 pieces of paper or index cards (Place at home, car, and work)

State- Speak with a powerful tone and total belief 3 times a day: Morning, Evening, and Before bed.

Meditate- Think about affirmations at least 8 times (exercising, walking, driving, eating, working, etc.).

*14 interactions with the Daily Affirmations = a person's average of 450,000 daily thoughts.

Enthusiasm
Affirmations

Saturday

I vigorously seek finding ways to bless
other people.
I find ways to be a blessing to
other people.
I always put effort in being a blessing
to other people.

Affirmation Instructions:

Write- Record Daily Affirmations on *3* pieces of paper or index cards (Place at home, car, and work)

State- Speak with a powerful tone and total belief *3* times a day: Morning, Evening, and Before bed.

Meditate- Think about affirmations at least *8* times (exercising, walking, driving, eating, working, etc.).

*14 interactions with the Daily Affirmations = a person's average of 450,000 daily thoughts.

Enthusiasm Affirmations

Sunday

I am passionate about having joy, peace, and happiness.
Joy, peace, and happiness are what I am passionate about.
My passion is linked to joy, peace, and happiness.

5. Network

Romans 14:19 (NIV) Let us therefore make every effort to do what leads to peace and to mutual edification.

What is Networking?

Yes, I know that we all have jobs and are working to provide for ourselves and family, working hard to pay bills. Are you networking for a career change, job promotion, or entrepreneurship development? Typically, most of us define networking as going to an event and passing out business cards to promote our brand or business. My definition is little different than that: *Networking* is a proactive approach to meet, learn, and collaborate with other people to help them and yourself. I just believe that when you help other people, those same people will help you in return. That is why networking is so important. Networking is the mother-ship to birth solid business relationships, personal mentorships, and ownership of your purpose potential.

Working Your Network

I have proof that networking can lead to promotion. Yes, every job that I have obtained in my life came from my skills and knowledge, but it also came from networking. There are three things I did to guarantee that I had a solid and large network to help me throughout my life and career. Simply support others, consistently search for options, and connect to be the best.

Simply Support Others

The first thing to grow an effective network is to simply support others. That means you are providing support and encouragement. I remember when I worked at a Nissan Dealership, my friend Steve worked at a Toyota dealership. My first couple of months I only averaged selling 3-4 cars, while Steve averaged car sales of 5 per month. We both were short of the national average for salesman of 10 cars per month. We both were at risk of losing our jobs because we were falling short of our company goals. Then it dawned on me that neither one of us was supporting each other. We had a solid friendship but we needed to build a strong business network. So I came up with the plan that if we worked together we could double our efforts.

Double Your Effort = Double Your Results

The goal was for us both to sell 10 cars each month. Your goal may be to complete all your classes to get a college degree. Network with other students with the same major/classes to improve your GPA. Your goal is to lose 20 pounds, so network with a gym buddy. The goal is to help other people by working with them, and they in return will help you to reach your goal. Back to the story. Yes, I sold 3-4 cars a month, but I had at least 20 applications per month. I revisited those files, and I noticed that most applicants opted to leave the question blank that asked if they had other car preferences. I made one phone call and asked a lady did she have preferences besides a Nissan and she said, "Toyota." Immediately I said, "My friend Steve who works at Toyota can help you purchase your new car." Steve and I decided to combine our efforts to get maximum results. We combined all the rejected applications to prequalify their credit, income, and readiness to purchase a new Nissan or Toyota vehicle.

Every time I had customers that preferred a Toyota instead of a Nissan, I would contact Steve to give him a customer lead. I referred the customer to him, and they purchased the car. My friend was satisfied and the customer was satisfied. I supported him and in return whenever he had customers that wanted a Nissan instead of a Toyota he referred them to me. All the customers that I referred to Steve even referred people to me. Steve and I shared our leads to accomplish success. For 8 months straight we both sold 10 plus cars a month through building a solid networking relationship. Who can you network with to increase your sales? What alternatives can you think of to increase your production at work? Who can you assist that can help you? Creating your network helps someone else and in return, they will help you.

Search For Options

Networking opens the windows of options/opportunities. Go to events where people of the same interest, skills, or profession congregate. Form new relationships. If you desire a promotion, thoroughly examine your options. Is there an option to apply for a position that you lack the certification or training needed? Can you transfer to another store or location? What higher level position matches your skills and talents? In searching for options to fulfill your desire, networking is the key concept. Afterwards, set up a meeting with your manager to discuss your future with the company. This is the greatest networking event you will ever attend and you're the host. Make your manager comfortable by discussing attributes you like the most about their management style. Proceed to give detailed information about the things you like about the company. You have the manager's attention, and then you pitch to your manager that you're in the position to help him to advance to the next promotional level of the company. The manager and you devise a plan of action to help your manager get promoted. I know this plan sounds awkward, but your primary focus is to network to the top. What manager would not be impressed with your humble suggestion to help them get promoted? When there is an open window of opportunity for your manager, it stays open for you too. In actuality your manager is training and equipping you to take over his current position even though you may not have enough experience or training. As you're training your manager for his promotion, you're getting hands on training to get promoted to your manager's current position.

What others will not do, you do for you. Please understand most employees will help themselves first before helping someone else. There is high probability for you to get a recommendation for promotion from your manager. Networking creates automatic promotion. Because of networking you have unlimited options for career advancement. You have the strength and skill to open the window of opportunities for job transfer, professional development, or promotion to management. You must continue to work your network. Don't be shy; try to network with people in higher positions that help you advance to the next level. Become comfortable building solid networks of relationships. As you move toward networking more, new relationships and promotions start approaching you.

It is time for transitioning to the next level in your life. It is going to require you to network. Network to find the ideal opportunity that you're looking for in life and get to where you're going. Open your mouth then share your vision and purpose. Meet new people and give the new information about what you have learned. Search outside of your comfort zone to get in the comfortable place of success, significance, and strong support. Search externally from your current job to find your niche (what you're the best at doing). There is more for you! There is more in store for you! Build your network.

Find a community where everyone has the same mindset and similar skills. The community is accountable for pushing you to develop your talents and gifts. Friendly competition where everyone supports each other to become their best. can be quite beneficial. A good example would be for you meet at least 5 new people every week, that are in your field and other positions that you are trying to pursue in your life. See what happens. Success, promotion, new relationships, happiness, and income increase. It is all about networking, building relationships, and connecting with other people daily. You can Network!!

Connect To Be The B.E.S.T.

Are you connecting with other people?
Do you see consistent promotion?
Are you accelerating in your life?
Are you really operating in your full potential?

Come correct to connect to be the B.E.S.T. Yes, you have confidence in your skills. You have confidence in your knowledge. You have confidence in your abilities. Do you have all the confidence in your purpose? I believe that connecting with other people is essential in propelling you into purpose. Connecting with other people is very important for your promotion and for your growth/development in life. Connecting with other people builds up your worth. It gives you the momentum you need to capture moments of walking in success through the shoes of others. Connecting with other people makes you better because it adds new perspectives, improves knowledge, and trains you for success. You need other people to be successful. Who wants to succeed alone? No one. Be significant to your spouse and kids. Be financially independent. Connect to achieve all your goals and dreams. To be your best you need help. Connect to be the best.

The greatest joy as a parent is connecting with your child, teaching them about risks and rewards, and choices and consequences. The parent is the teacher, and the child is the student who is learning at a fast pace. The child follows the parent's advice and instructions. The child trusts and believes the parents know what they're talking about. That is how you need to be as an adult. We have to connect with other people to get to where we are trying to go.

Relationships are built to give you security of a bright future. Your goal is to be always exposed to experiencing new things. Get first hand knowledge in relationships by asking critical questions about faith, finances, health, and dreams. This builds trust in the relationship. Find people that know more than you about a particular subject and are willing to share advice on their successes and failures. Now you have their knowledge, experience, and expertise at your fingertips. You becoming your best is the end result of connecting with other people. Your knowledge is accelerated to reach your potential with valuable advice on life and business insight. Experience, knowledge, and understanding enable you to have direct participation in repeating the process of success that was done before you by others. Networking gives you guided instructions on you operating in purpose and reaching maximum potential. You're building multiple networks for your professional, personal, and spiritual growth. Now you know exactly what your next move is going to be. You seek new ideas. Make an effort and attempt to push yourself to discover innovative ways to become successful. Trust again. You must expect and wish to receive a benefit from someone else. The bridge where you are today to where you are trying to go tomorrow is based on you connecting with other people. Job promotion, acceleration in knowledge, advancement by experiences, increase in income, and valuable self-worth are all based on connecting with other people. I declare and decree new relationships. I declare and decree that everything that you touch will prosper. I declare and decree an enlarged mindset that gives a clear path for your purpose and potential.

Aim For Your Promotion

Do you want a promotion this year? Why do you deserve a promotion? When do you want a promotion this year? It can happen for you this year if you aim high. In any season, you can set your goals on hitting the target of promotion. The five ways to aim for promotion are **research, development, visualization, praying,** and **petitioning.**

First thing you must do is **research**. Research all the available positions at your current company, especially the positions that have a higher salary or require more responsibilities than your current position. Now, research your ideal job title and duties including the salary. Find out information on the four previous individuals who were selected for this position. Compare your skills with their skills. Post a copy of this new job promotion in your bathroom, car, and wallet. Read and study the details of this job every morning, evening, and night.

Next, you need **development** in the researched position that you're seeking. Sign up for classes or get the training needed to get this promotion. I recommend personal and professional development for your next promotion because your main goal is to do this job better than anyone has ever done before. Take advantage of studying YouTube videos or taking online courses. Ask the previous people who held this position if they can network with you to give you advice and training tips to help you succeed at this job.

Also, you must **visualize** yourself going to the interview. What are you going to wear? What questions are you going to ask? Visualize yourself shaking the employer's hand as you're getting the promotion. Visualize you effectively completing the job duties. Visualize your first paycheck and the increase in your pay. Visualize your bank account having more money in it. Rehearse in your mind the whole networking process to get the new job.

In addition, you must **pray** and speak affirmations. Get with your spouse, family, and friends to start praying about the promotion in advance. Pray all during the day, every day. Express affirmations in the morning and look directly in the mirror and say "I am promoted"; "I see increase in my salary". Pray and speak affirmations for your promotion.

Lastly, you must **petition** for your new position before other candidates. Set up your own interview. Meet with your manager or supervisor to give notice that you're ready for promotion. Petition for your new position because you're well informed, properly prepared, and skill ready. You're so familiar with the duties and skills needed for the new job that you are comfortable in the interview. Your manager or supervisor is impressed with your knowledge. Perfectly aim at your promotion with research, development, visualization, praying, and petitioning for your new position.

NETWORK EMPIRE OF 10

1. The Mentee: This is a person you assist in reaching their career goals and lifelong dreams. You're available for your mentee to give support and encouragement if needed. You have an empathetic heart for your mentee because they remind you of yourself. As you're helping your mentee, it motivates you to do even better for yourself.

Possible Mentees: _____

_____   _____

2. The Supporter: You both share a common interest or similar goals. Sometimes there is a lot of sharing going on because you both are going through the same thing at the same time. With this sharing there comes a great level of mutual understanding and support when good and bad things happen. Supporters share sources of information and helpful advice.

Possible Supporters: _____

_____   _____

3. The Innovator: The innovator is always seeking to discover a new and more effective way of doing something. They always have plans to create and discover things. When you're in their presence, you feel tremendously inspired. They are valuable resources to help you set goals.

Possible Innovators: _____

_____   _____

4. The Optimist: This person is always looking at the positive in any situation. They believe in giving you their honest opinion and genuine correction. They give you the push to continue your dreams despite setbacks or failures.

Possible Optimists: _____

_____   _____

5. The Idealist: You network with this person to help with formulating an action plan for your dreams. The idealist find a way to still help you stay on track to reach your dream even though you do not have a strategic plan for success. They give you ideal ways to achieve your dreams.

Possible Idealists: _____

_____ _____

6. The Social Connector: This person gives you easy access to people who can help you with budgeting finances, career changes, relationship advice, entrepreneurship resources, etc.; helps you to build relationships and find opportunities so you can obtain your career and entrepreneurship goals; and assists you in coming up with a plan to use social media to gain leverage on prosperity and operating in your purpose.

Possible Social Connectors: _____

_____ _____

7. The Pioneer: They are currently doing things that have never been done before. Even though pioneers have a different area of expertise than you, there is still a mutual respect to work together. Their philosophies and accomplishments intrigue you. It benefits you to network with pioneers because they can help create reachable goals from a different perspective.

Possible Pioneers: _____

_____ _____

8. The Source: This person knows everything about current trends and old trends in the workforce. This is a good person to share dreams and ideas with so they can point you into the right direction. The Source has information, resources, and people who can help you aim for achievement.

Possible Sources: _____

_____ _____

9. The Coach: The coach is there for your personal needs and business to have a bright future. This is going to motivate, inspire, and train you to move from one place to another. Coaches give constructive criticism and helpful insight. Coaches help with you create your next best move.

Possible Coaches: _____

_____   _____

10. The Mentor: This person shows consistent accomplishments in achieving goals. Mentors assist in training you to become successful. Mentors always share pertinent information and vital resources. They give you a good game plan to win at everything.

Possible Mentors: _____

_____   _____

You can have unlimited potential at your fingertips by building a diverse network of people to help you professionally, spiritually, financially, and socially. It is critical that you network to create partnerships where both parties can benefit from the connection. Some network connections may be only for a season, but still seek to find a replacement. Your success can't be completed alone; you have to connect with other people. Your Network Empire of 10 is not limited by race, age, gender, financial status, or backgrounds. Professional development and business ventures solely depend on who is in your network empire.

N.E.T.W.O.R.K.

*What's your secret weapon for your career advancement?

One foolproof way to impact your career for the long-term is to develop and maintain a vast network of contacts. The benefits of establishing a strong network for your career are seemingly endless. Here are just a few to consider if you're looking to boost your career with the foundation of networking:

NAVIGATE - For your career, job, or business, navigation is key. Where do you want to be in the future? What is your ideal job? Structure your network to consist of people who will welcome and share good advice for your career goals. This network consists of business mentors who are willing to sacrifice their time to instill in you the drive, will, and guidance needed to accomplish your purpose. This network safely and carefully directs your transition to another company and promotion to another job title. Managers, supervisors, executives, and entrepreneurs are ideal candidates for this network.

EXPLORE - Go to forums, meetings, groups, and seminars that relate to your career and social ambitions. Your goal is to learn something new about something you know very little of. Hopefully, by networking with different people you can discover a new interest that is out of your comfort zone. Connect with unique individuals to have access to information to help you become more innovative. Depend on others to learn new skills and techniques so you can embrace change. Group leaders, supporters, and event coordinators are ideal candidates for this network.

TENDENCY TO GROW - Consistent personal and professional development is important to you achieving your goals. Always share your goals with people who can help you. This creates accountability in your ability to grow. The element of support encourages you to study harder and longer on reaching your goals. Invest in workshops, seminars, and training to improve your knowledge and skills. You need that extra push to try, apply, and never be denied of an opportunity for promotion or advancement. Spouse, family, friends, coworkers, and even your boss are ideal candidates for this network.

WORTH - You have a great worth of knowledge. Your central focus is to build personal and professional relationships with business leaders who have accomplished things that you desire. Your network of friends and associates are a part of your worth. These networks can open doors that once were closed because of who you now know. Your name becomes attached to your network. You have power and worth because of who you have connected with. Business leaders, branch managers, and regional managers are ideal candidates for this network.

OPTION - Always be willing to be humble and sacrifice. Even if a particular job may overlook your skills and talents you can still build a solid relationship with that company. Options always lead to opportunity. A great thing you can do is to volunteer your services, talents, or skills to assist the company you desire to work in. Volunteer at company held seminar, appreciation luncheon, golf tournament, fundraiser program, or award ceremony. Keep in touch with the event coordinator to be the first to volunteer. Now you have access to the hiring managers and human resource department. Be the best volunteer and get noticed for your work ethics. Have engaging conversations and thought provoking questions. Make sure you stand out as a volunteer in hopes of getting a job interview. Have faith, use the option to volunteer, and stand out. Hiring managers and human resource personnel are ideal candidates for this network.

RESOURCE - Organize your vast network of people to be broken down into different categories. Now you have an arsenal of contacts, mentors, and business leaders that are available to help your dream become a reality. Keep in contact with them regularly for advice and meetings. Resources of networking must be kept relevant, fresh, and familiar. Therefore, you will be the first person called for new opportunities because you worked your network.

KNOW WHO TO CALL - Sometimes life is tough and you experience setbacks. Your greatest comeback is your network for advice, wisdom, and direction. Once your network is built, it will always be available, valuable, and professional to you. A solid network mutually benefits all parties involved. One phone call, one meeting, and one discussion with your network can get you back on track to your destiny and purpose.

Affirmation Instructions:

Write- Record Daily Affirmations on 3 pieces of paper or index cards (Place at home, car, and work)

State- Speak with a powerful tone and total belief 3 times a day: Morning, Evening, and Before bed.

Meditate- Think about affirmations at least 8 times (exercising, walking, driving, eating, working, etc.).

*14 interactions with the Daily Affirmations = a person's average of 450,000 daily thoughts.

Network Affirmations

Monday

I use my gifts to connect with other gifted people.

Other gifted people connect with my gifts.

To connect with other gifted people I use my gift.

Affirmation Instructions:

Write- Record Daily Affirmations on 3 pieces of paper or index cards (Place at home, car, and work)

State- Speak with a powerful tone and total belief 3 times a day: Morning, Evening, and Before bed.

Meditate- Think about affirmations at least 8 times (exercising, walking, driving, eating, working, etc.).

*14 interactions with the Daily Affirmations = a person's average of 450,000 daily thoughts.

<u>Network Affirmations</u>

Tuesday

I choose only "Success" to be on my team.
The only thing on my team is "Success".
My team of choice is "Success".

Affirmation Instructions:

Write- Record Daily Affirmations on *3* pieces of paper or index cards (Place at home, car, and work)

State- Speak with a powerful tone and total belief *3* times a day: Morning, Evening, and Before bed.

Meditate- Think about affirmations at least *8* times (exercising, walking, driving, eating, working, etc.).

*14 interactions with the Daily Affirmations = a person's average of 450,000 daily thoughts.

Network Affirmations

Wednesday

I share my vision with like
minded people.
My vision is shared by like
minded people.
Like minded people share
my vision.

Affirmation Instructions:

Write- Record Daily Affirmations on 3 pieces of paper or index cards (Place at home, car, and work)

State- Speak with a powerful tone and total belief 3 times a day: Morning, Evening, and Before bed.

Meditate- Think about affirmations at least 8 times (exercising, walking, driving, eating, working, etc.).

*14 interactions with the Daily Affirmations = a person's average of 450,000 daily thoughts.

Network
Affirmations

Thursday

The ladder of success links up the
right people.
The right people are linked on the
ladder of success.
Success is a ladder that links the
right people together.

Affirmation Instructions:

Write- Record Daily Affirmations on 3 pieces of paper or index cards (Place at home, car, and work)

State- Speak with a powerful tone and total belief 3 times a day: Morning, Evening, and Before bed.

Meditate- Think about affirmations at least 8 times (exercising, walking, driving, eating, working, etc.).

*14 interactions with the Daily Affirmations = a person's average of 450,000 daily thoughts.

Network Affirmations

Friday

I embrace positive feedback from important people in my life.
It is important that I embrace positive feedback from others.
I embrace others who give me positive feedback.

Affirmation Instructions:

Write- Record Daily Affirmations on 3 pieces of paper or index cards (Place at home, car, and work)

State- Speak with a powerful tone and total belief 3 times a day: Morning, Evening, and Before bed.

Meditate- Think about affirmations at least 8 times (exercising, walking, driving, eating, working, etc.).

*14 interactions with the Daily Affirmations = a person's average of 450,000 daily thoughts.

Network Affirmations

Saturday

I build solid business relationships on social media.
My business builds solid relationships on social media.
Social media can build solid business relationships.

Affirmation Instructions:

Write- Record Daily Affirmations on 3 pieces of paper or index cards (Place at home, car, and work)

State- Speak with a powerful tone and total belief 3 times a day: Morning, Evening, and Before bed.

Meditate- Think about affirmations at least 8 times (exercising, walking, driving, eating, working, etc.).

*14 interactions with the Daily Affirmations = a person's average of 450,000 daily thoughts.

Network Affirmations

Sunday

I network with successful people who do what I desire.
I desire to network with successful people.
My desired success requires me to network.

6. Time Management

Luke 14:28 ESV. For which you, desiring to build a tower, does not first sit down and count the cost, whether he has enough to complete it?

Time is a Valuable Commodity

You know the key to time management. I am going to be honest with you. I have been struggling with time management. Husband, father, deacon, dean of students, teacher, author, owner of a clothing line, public speaker…it has been a struggle juggling this time management. So many tasks must be completed in a limited amount of time. Time is a valuable commodity because it is priceless, precious, and promising. Use these three keys – pause, manage, and permit – to unlock time management.

Pause T.I.M.E.

One of the greatest questions you can ever ask a person is can you pause time? The obvious answer is NO. Through research, I discovered that time is a continuous event that travels the future, present, and past. In a day there are 24 hours, 14,404 minutes, and 86,400 seconds. Even though time cannot be paused, a person can take a break away or stop doing a certain task in a day to get a better hold on time. Time is elusive to most people sometimes because time goes slow when people are bored and time goes fast when people are having fun. Your objective is to find ways to press a temporary pause on time so you can complete all your daily tasks.

Manage T.I.M.E.

Time is constant and consistent. You have no control over time unless you have the time keys. For individuals to be good at time management, they must have one control factor. What can a person control that is related to time? A key component of time management is to be better at managing yourself through technology, invest in automation, multiply efforts, and efficient application.

Permit T.IM.E.

Something is lacking in time management when there is a desk full of uncompleted work. Give yourself permission to work on something today and you will have more time for tomorrow. Everyone has a cell phone, laptop, iPad, iPod, or computer. Why is technology not used as a tool for better time management? You can email, text, video conference, create documents, and add a signature all at the same time through most technology. Therefore, concentrate on doing multiple things at the same time by using technology. The days for licking stamps to mail out bill payments are over. The days of standing in line on Friday for a whole hour to cash or deposit your check are over.

Invest in automation, to have online bill pay or electronic direct deposit. Everything you do should be automated because it saves countless amounts of time. Delegate tasks to other people or set specific times to complete tasks so your efforts can be multiplied. You don't waste time; you chase time to catch up on all your tasks. With efficient application, tasks are completed correctly the first time. Effectively manage yourself and time. You are a great manager of time. You complete all your tasks for tomorrow today, therefore you are ahead. You are effective and productive with managing your time.

Are you late turning in assignments?
Do you get enough sleep at night?
Do you occasionally miss deadlines?
Are you behind checking your emails or texts?
Do you find yourself stuck with incomplete tasks?
Do you procrastinate and things just pile up instantly?

14 Time Tricks That Stick Productivity

1. **3:00 a.m. Grind** - Work on your business, dreams, or goals. While everybody is sleeping, you are up Grinding. Create advertisements, post on social media, check emails, pray, or read for

self improvement. You have a 4-6 hour head start against other people in the world.

2. **5:00 a.m. Workout** - Wake your mind and body up early in the morning so they both can perform at maximum capacity. This adrenaline transfers creativity to your mind and productivity by planning your work.

3. **Goal Sheet** - Use index cards or sheets of paper to list 5-10 goals that you must complete today. Put your goal sheet in key places in your life and seek to complete them by any means necessary. Draw a line through completed goals.

4. **Calendar** - Write down date sensitive things to remember on a calendar. Refer to the calendar all day to stay on track and be productive. Have an updated list of appointments, meetings, calls, conferences, phone numbers, names, email addresses on a desk calendar. Your calendar is a helpful resource and reference to maximize your time management.

5. **Maximize Time** - Find those free moments during the day to do something relating to your dream, purpose, or goals. Multi-task minor tasks periodically as the day progresses. Return a text while walking, check emails at lunch, or read in a traffic jam. Maximize your time when you have free time.

6. **Purposeful Breaks** - Intentionally plan breaks after completing goals. Relax and reflect. Breaks reduce stress and recharge your motivation to be productive. While on this purposeful break, still make plans for other uncompleted tasks.

7. **Motivating Words** - These two words motivate you to accomplish anything: *Complete and*

Start. Every time you finish a task, mark it with "Complete" and state out loud "Complete". You experience great joy when a task is completed. Then next thing on your to-do-list is say out loud "Start". If you start strong you can finish strong. No matter if you have delays, setbacks, or bad outcomes still say "Complete" or "Start".

8. Check Off Inbox/Text - In today's business world, your email or phone is linked to your communication with past and potential business. Make sure all emails and texts are read carefully and completely. Immediately respond to keep the momentum of productivity going. Also, delete old unimportant email or texts to free up storage space and increase the speed of correspondence.

9. Turn Off Electronic Devices - When you have to meet deadlines or a major project is due, be sure to avoid all distractions. During these critical times, focus on the task at hand by turning off all electronic devices. Fewer distractions help you become more productive.

10. Weekend Work - Be proactive in planning the upcoming week. Set aside time during Saturday or Sunday to work on tasks relating to your job or business. Doing work in one hour increments help increase productivity for upcoming week.

11. Study Biographies - In your spare time, read or watch movies that are biographies of famous people. Sometimes the stories are similar to your story. These biographies can add inspiration for your purpose. The biographies sometimes replay how people overcame great odds to pursue their purpose. In most biographies, productivity and time management is a key point of discussion. What is your own biography? List all the life lessons you have learned about better time management.

12. **Delegate** - You need help to complete your workload. The power in delegating specific tasks to other people is for some of the workload to taken off of you. Always, delegate to selective people who have the skill, experience, and right attitude to perform well. Management of tasks becomes easier when delegation is a part of completing tasks.

13. **Set Alarms -** Be mindful to set alarms on watches, clocks, emails, and other devices to become more productive. The alarm tells when to start or finish a task. The alarms keep your production on time.

14. **Master Life -** Take time every day and study your life. Look at all the components: family, career, spirit, dreams, business, health, finances, etc. Next, manage them well, update when needed, and ask for help sometimes. You can master your life and get maximum results by studying your life.

Time Management Questionnaire

Scoring: **2** = Always **1** = Sometimes **0** = Never

- I complete things in order of priority _____
- All day, I complete what needs to be done ___
- I complete my assignments/tasks on time _____
- I use my time effectively _____
- No delays with difficult and unpleasant tasks___
- I force myself to plan my time _____
- I create a daily and weekly goal sheet _____
- My priority list is in order of importance _____
- I meet deadlines, no last minute rushing____
- I am current on my research & development___
- I have no interruptions for high priority tasks__
- I don't waste time on trivial matters _____
- I spend enough time on work-related activities__
- I weekly schedule relaxation & family time___
- I keep a record of fixed commitments ___
- I complete important tasks with more energy___
- I use driving, walking, or eating as free time to complete tasks _____
- I often compare my activities to my goals_____
- I stop all wasteful or unprofitable routines_____
- I screen and control my telephone calls/text ___
- I set alerts to start & complete tasks on phone/email__
- I plan activities in advance_____
- I delegate tasks to avoid work overload_____
- I write on daily calendar to manage time___
- I GRIND at 3am-5am to stay ahead of time___

Results

45 to 50: Outstanding time management skills

38 to 44: Strong time management skills

30 to 37: You are managing your time fairly well, but sometimes feel overwhelmed.

25 to 36: Stressful and less than satisfying of time management for work, career, family.

Less than 25: Need to work on time management

Early Success Schedule

**Wake up early to work on goals and vision
while other people are asleep.
Grind between 3:00 a.m. to 5:00 a.m.,
depending on your daily schedule.**

Exercise your body - Energy

Adjustment of mental attitude - Focus

Read the word of God aloud - Inspiration

Listen for guidance from mentor – A Plan

Yesterday recap - Reflection

Body, Mind, Voice, Hear, Discover

Daily G.R.I.N.D.

(Generate Repeated Improvements To Nurture Your Dreams)

Grind Time   Momentum Activity   Learn

3:00 A.M. *

4:00 A.M. *

5:00 A.M. *

6:00 A.M.

7:00 A.M.

8:00 A.M.

9:00 A.M.

10:00 A.M

11:00 A.M.

12:00 P.M.

1:00 P.M.

2:00 P.M.

3:00 P.M.

4:00 P.M.

5:00 P.M.

*Pray, Check emails, Social Media, Exercise,
YouTube, Videos, Market your company, etc.

Affirmation Instructions:

Write- Record Daily Affirmations on 3 pieces of paper or index cards (Place at home, car, and work)

State- Speak with a powerful tone and total belief 3 times a day: Morning, Evening, and Before bed.

Meditate- Think about affirmations at least 8 times (exercising, walking, driving, eating, working, etc.).

*14 interactions with the Daily Affirmations = a person's average of 450,000 daily thoughts.

Time Management Affirmations

Monday

I schedule my dates of success with great time management.
With great time management, I schedule my dates of success.
My success dates are scheduled with great time management.

Affirmation Instructions:

Write- Record Daily Affirmations on *3* pieces of paper or index cards (Place at home, car, and work)

State- Speak with a powerful tone and total belief *3* times a day: Morning, Evening, and Before bed.

Meditate- Think about affirmations at least *8* times (exercising, walking, driving, eating, working, etc.).

*14 interactions with the Daily Affirmations = a person's average of 450,000 daily thoughts.

Time Management

Affirmations

Tuesday

In my free time, I create my perfect life.
The creation of my perfect life happens
in my free time.
I find free time to create my
perfect life.

Affirmation Instructions:

Write- Record Daily Affirmations on *3* pieces of paper or index cards (Place at home, car, and work)

State- Speak with a powerful tone and total belief *3* times a day: Morning, Evening, and Before bed.

Meditate- Think about affirmations at least *8* times (exercising, walking, driving, eating, working, etc.).

*14 interactions with the Daily Affirmations = a person's average of 450,000 daily thoughts.

Time Management Affirmations

Wednesday

My goals and vision have targeted dates of completion.

I set target dates of completion for my goals and vision.

My goal is to set target dates of completion for my vision.

Affirmation Instructions:

Write- Record Daily Affirmations on *3* pieces of paper or index cards (Place at home, car, and work)

State- Speak with a powerful tone and total belief *3* times a day: Morning, Evening, and Before bed.

Meditate- Think about affirmations at least *8* times (exercising, walking, driving, eating, working, etc.).

*14 interactions with the Daily Affirmations = a person's average of 450,000 daily thoughts.

Time Management Affirmations

Thursday

I find time to make life improvements through visualization.

Visualization is my time to make life improvements.

Improvements in my life are discovered during visualization time.

Affirmation Instructions:

Write- Record Daily Affirmations on *3* pieces of paper or index cards (Place at home, car, and work)

State- Speak with a powerful tone and total belief *3* times a day: Morning, Evening, and Before bed.

Meditate- Think about affirmations at least *8* times (exercising, walking, driving, eating, working, etc.).

*14 interactions with the Daily Affirmations = a person's average of 450,000 daily thoughts.

Time Management Affirmations

Friday

I complete all tasks quickly and efficiently.

All my tasks are completed quickly and efficiently.

Quickly and efficiently, all my tasks are completed.

Affirmation Instructions:

Write- Record Daily Affirmations on 3 pieces of paper or index cards (Place at home, car, and work)

State- Speak with a powerful tone and total belief 3 times a day: Morning, Evening, and Before bed.

Meditate- Think about affirmations at least 8 times (exercising, walking, driving, eating, working, etc.).

*14 interactions with the Daily Affirmations = a person's average of 450,000 daily thoughts.

Time Management

Affirmations

Saturday

Every day I create a priority list.

Create a daily priority list.

My priority list is created daily.

Affirmation Instructions:

Write- Record Daily Affirmations on *3* pieces of paper or index cards (Place at home, car, and work)

State- Speak with a powerful tone and total belief *3* times a day: Morning, Evening, and Before bed.

Meditate- Think about affirmations at least *8* times (exercising, walking, driving, eating, working, etc.).

*14 interactions with the Daily Affirmations = a person's average of 450,000 daily thoughts.

Time Management Affirmations

Sunday

I arrive at every appointment early.

Every appointment I arrive early.

I arrive early to all my appointments.

7. Uniqueness

<u>Psalms 139:14 (ESV).</u> I praise You, for I am fearfully and wonderfully made. Wonderful are Your works; my soul knows it very well.

Embrace Your Uniqueness

We know that we are all different. The way we talk, walk, look, and how we relate to each other makes us unique. To be unique means to be rare, special, and one of a kind where there are no equals. There is a struggle *sometimes* in embracing your uniqueness.

Test Your Uniqueness

I struggled with embracing my uniqueness because of outside forces. Can other people tell you how to embrace your uniqueness? When I first started teaching middle school math, I was doing a great job. The kids got excited and engaged in learning math. Strangely, I had one teacher to come up to me and say, "Mr. Momon you smile too much and the kids will not take you seriously because you are smiling too much." Now this was a 20 year veteran teacher that said this. I had to make a decision to use *my uniqueness* or *her experience*. Like a FOOL, I chose *her* experience. Yes, I took the advice of the experienced teacher, and started teaching students with less smiling and more one on one interaction.

The Impact Of Uniqueness

I started teaching my kids about math without smiling. The kids asked, "Mr. Momon, are you OK? What is wrong with you, you're not smiling?" I said, "I am OK." This change did not get good results. Students reverted back to being unmotivated about learning math and their grades dropped dramatically. 85% of my students were failing my quizzes and tests. I had to go back to *my uniqueness*. I started smiling with lots of positive energy while teaching. Once again, the kids were having fun learning math, and they showed remarkable academic improvement. It was all because of the positive energy related to me teaching the math curriculum. Yes, I am animated in my teaching style! Yes, I smile a lot while teaching! Yes, I find creative ways for students to do physical activities and learn math concepts too! Yes, I think outside the box of traditional teaching styles! Yes, I allow students to have academic conversations during class to link social skills with learning! Yes, I sometimes mix a science experiment with learning a math formula, but it works for us.

After changing back to my unique qualities of teaching, the academic results improved again. All my students passed my math class. That is *my uniqueness*. Yes, I am animated, Yes, I am excited. Yes, I smile a lot, but that is *my uniqueness*. I use the hands-on approach to teaching. This is *my uniqueness*. What is your uniqueness? How do you flow in your uniqueness? I flow in *my uniqueness* and that is why my students are growing in knowledge of math. They benefit from me being me. I embrace everything unique about me, even if somebody has an issue with it. I love what I do, and continue to motivate whomever I come in contact with. Embrace your uniqueness. Embrace those things that make you stand out or set you apart from other people.

What Makes You Unique?

Quality	Value
Irreplaceable	It is difficult to find someone to replace your role and function at your job. You are the best at your position because you constantly seek training and development.
Invaluable	It is difficult to calculate your monetary worth potential. Your gifts and talents open you up for promotion and salary increases.
Indispensable	It is absolutely necessary for you to be involved in your spouse and children's lives. You share unconditional love with your family.
Indestructible	Your dreams can never be destroyed or derailed. *Your super passion is glued to your purpose.* They are inseparable.
Incomparable	It is impossible to compare your contribution to your family, church, job, and community. You are unique in your own way.
Immeasurable	It is impossible to measure your wisdom, knowledge, and understanding. Your mind is always open to learning something new.

Embrace who you are and then you can go far. The time is now. Divine completeness happens because of your uniqueness. You're unique and distinct. Embrace your uniqueness today, so nobody can stop you from experiencing your desired life.

Worth and value is based on how you use your uniqueness. What do you think you are worth? Do you think you are worth more than your coworkers? God gives us gifts, talents, skills, and uniqueness that have to be groomed for growth for you to experience your true potential. You have to make a choice to be like the average person or to be who God has called you to be.

Discover Your Unique Purpose

Did you know that God created each person with a bunch of unique qualities? Some qualities people are naturally born with and some qualities people have to develop or discover over time. Do you want to discover the unique qualities that God has blessed you with? These unique qualities were created to help you develop your potential and accomplish your purpose. We all have similar talents and skills, but the difference is God has given us all a certain amount of potential to fulfill our divine purpose. For example, most basketball players can use their hands to dribble and shoot a basketball, but they do not have the work ethics, accuracy, and success that Michael Jordan had during his career. That is why you have to discover your uniqueness along with God's purpose for you.

Unique Profile

Do you believe you're Great? Does your life match what you think about yourself? Is there anything great about being average? No!! People that have found their purpose and ran with passion, conviction, obedience, and integrity have succeeded. It does not matter where you start; what matters is you work today to be Great in the future. Take President Barack Obama and Michael Jackson, for instance. Society says you have to be born rich to be an achiever or you have to get all A's in school and have a college degree to be successful. Neither President Obama nor Michael Jackson was born rich nor had excellent academic achievement. Yet, they both achieved world renowned success! Their purpose, path, and plan were different, and so is yours. God has already planned your purpose, you just have to stay near, believe, and execute the divine plan that

God gives to you. Social media says you are famous because of how many followers you have and the likes on your pictures or posts. Your main goal is to know that you were already created with a unique profile that consists of one of a kind skills and talents. Your main goal is to grow from mediocrity to achieving unique success in all fields of human endeavors. Use your uniqueness by any means necessary to achieve your greatness.

Time To Develop

Your makeup is unique, distinct, and extraordinary. You are better than average. Everything you do, say, or think makes you stand out among others. Develop your skills and talents to enable you to fulfill God's purpose. The successful, unsuccessful, ordinary, and unmotivated all have the exact same 24 hours per day to accomplish their goals. All time is the same for everybody, but how you manage time along with talent makes you unique.

Look Inside To Be Unique

Are you stuck in a place of doubting your abilities? Do you get overwhelmed with many tasks because of procrastination? Even kids can discover their unique hidden qualities, if parents allow them to freely express themselves and have more patience with interpreting failures. This is another opportunity to find purpose and success. Today, leave your comfort zone so unfamiliar things can be transformed into something great. This world is fast paced and competitive. Look deep inside yourself for the knowledge you need to succeed at being unique. Use one unique thing to make a positive difference in people's lives. Stay connected with people who support you, teach you, and bring out your unique qualities that make you great.

Draw Out Your
U.N.I.Q.U.E.N.E.S.S.

Understand Your Great Potential - Develop character and integrity.

Never Stop Thinking Differently – Think outside the box. Present different thoughts to the world.

Investigate God's Plans - Study the bible to discover what God has next for you.

Quality Of Work - Take pride in your work. Have the best attitude and effort.

Utilize Gifts & Talents - Consistently attend training and personal development workshops. Cultivate your gifts and talents to be used in appropriate places.

Expect The Best - God's Vision for you is to stay motivated. Your dream is the truth about you.

Next Move Is Already Planned- Stay on the Purpose course. No derailment or distractions.

Explore Yourself - Find clues about yourself through asking other people how they see you.

Student For Life - Always be open to learn from other people. Look at everything as a teachable moment. Work hard by researching to find your uniqueness.

Submit to Spiritual Authority - Follow advice of spiritual leadership.

Affirmation Instructions:

Write- Record Daily Affirmations on *3* pieces of paper or index cards (Place at home, car, and work)

State- Speak with a powerful tone and total belief *3* times a day: Morning, Evening, and Before bed.

Meditate- Think about affirmations at least *8* times (exercising, walking, driving, eating, working, etc.).

*14 interactions with the Daily Affirmations = a person's average of 450,000 daily thoughts.

Uniqueness Affirmations

Monday

I love and respect the truths of myself and others.

The truth of myself and others is loved and respected by me.

The truth about me is I love and respect others.

Affirmation Instructions:

Write- Record Daily Affirmations on 3 pieces of paper or index cards (Place at home, car, and work)

State- Speak with a powerful tone and total belief 3 times a day: Morning, Evening, and Before bed.

Meditate- Think about affirmations at least 8 times (exercising, walking, driving, eating, working, etc.).

*14 interactions with the Daily Affirmations = a person's average of 450,000 daily thoughts.

Uniqueness Affirmations

Tuesday

I have the approval to fulfill my unique life purpose.

The fulfillment of my unique life purpose is approved.

My unique life purpose is approved and fulfilled.

Affirmation Instructions:

Write- Record Daily Affirmations on *3* pieces of paper or index cards (Place at home, car, and work)

State- Speak with a powerful tone and total belief *3* times a day: Morning, Evening, and Before bed.

Meditate- Think about affirmations at least *8* times (exercising, walking, driving, eating, working, etc.).

*14 interactions with the Daily Affirmations = a person's average of 450,000 daily thoughts.

<u>Uniqueness Affirmations</u>

Wednesday

My worthy cause is to give and bless others.

To give to and bless other people is

my worthy cause.

I am worthy because I give and bless others.

Affirmation Instructions:

Write- Record Daily Affirmations on 3 pieces of paper or index cards (Place at home, car, and work)

State- Speak with a powerful tone and total belief 3 times a day: Morning, Evening, and Before bed.

Meditate- Think about affirmations at least 8 times (exercising, walking, driving, eating, working, etc.).

*14 interactions with the Daily Affirmations = a person's average of 450,000 daily thoughts.

<u>Uniqueness Affirmations</u>

Thursday

My responsibility to my natural abilities is to be Great.

My natural ability is to have a responsibility in being Great.

I am Great because of my natural abilities and responsibility.

Affirmation Instructions:

Write- Record Daily Affirmations on *3* pieces of paper or index cards (Place at home, car, and work)

State- Speak with a powerful tone and total belief *3* times a day: Morning, Evening, and Before bed.

Meditate- Think about affirmations at least *8* times (exercising, walking, driving, eating, working, etc.).

*14 interactions with the Daily Affirmations = a person's average of 450,000 daily thoughts.

Uniqueness Affirmations

Friday

I have a unique talent, gift, and personality.

My talents, gifts, and personality are unique.

My uniqueness is my gifts, talents, and personality.

Affirmation Instructions:

Write- Record Daily Affirmations on *3* pieces of paper or index cards (Place at home, car, and work)

State- Speak with a powerful tone and total belief *3* times a day: Morning, Evening, and Before bed.

Meditate- Think about affirmations at least *8* times (exercising, walking, driving, eating, working, etc.).

*14 interactions with the Daily Affirmations = a person's average of 450,000 daily thoughts.

Uniqueness Affirmations

Saturday

Every day I appreciate my past, present, and future.

My past, present, and future are appreciated

by me every day.

I have an appreciation for my past, present, and

future.

Affirmation Instructions:

Write- Record Daily Affirmations on *3* pieces of paper or index cards (Place at home, car, and work)

State- Speak with a powerful tone and total belief *3* times a day: Morning, Evening, and Before bed.

Meditate- Think about affirmations at least *8* times (exercising, walking, driving, eating, working, etc.).

*14 interactions with the Daily Affirmations = a person's average of 450,000 daily thoughts.

Uniqueness Affirmations

Sunday

My difference is I make better changes, choices, and commitments.

Better changes, choices, and commitments make me different.

I make better changes, choices, and commitments; that is my difference.

8. Money Management

Proverbs 10:4. ESV. A slack hand causes poverty, but the hand of the diligent makes rich.

Discipline = Dollars

Your discipline equals more dollars. Yes, you want to be wealthy. Yes, you want to be prosperous. Yes, you want to be debt free. But my question to you is do you have discipline? Do you have financial discipline? So my job today is to teach you financial discipline. When I was going through transitioning from different jobs, I discovered a key reason why I was not successful financially. Just like most people, I struggled financially because I did not practice discipline in managing my finances. I kept avoiding simple basic biblical principles about prosperity, financial independence, and debt freedom. If you want more dollars, you need more discipline. There are nine ways a person can have discipline in their finances to maximize their income.

1. Budget

The first thing to help you achieve prosperity is budgeting. When you set up a budget, it will help you see your spending and saving patterns. You can't spend what you don't have. That is why it is important for you to have a working budget.

Set Up Your Budget

Bankrate.com states, "40% of Americans do not have a budget." Budgets can sometimes be a tedious and intimidating task that most people feel they can do without. On a monthly basis, most people struggle with not knowing where all their money goes and why they can't save any money. Having a budget is as important as making money. They work together giving an individual a clear financial picture of total bills, expenses, payments, and potential saving. Who would not want to know that?

Determine Income

First, you must live within your financial means to be able to afford your monthly expenses. Every time your income changes because of more hours or promotion, add the differences in the budget. Make notes in your budget that corresponds with monthly bills, if the frequency of your income varies from month to month. Set your budget accordingly if your income fluctuates because of commissions or bonuses. The budget key function is to let the consumer know the bottom line monthly amount they can spend, save, invest, and sow.

List Fixed Expenses

In your budget, list all your fixed expenses for every month. Fixed expenses (bills that are the same amount month to month) can include: mortgage, rent, car payment, student loan, tuition, car insurance, cable, utility bill, etc. Add a column for savings and tithes in the budget. Ideally you should automatically transfer 10% of your net income to a savings account, after making sure you can afford all bills. Reduce the amount owed on fixed expenses is the easiest method to reduce the monthly payments.

List Variable Expenses

In your budget, list all your variable expenses. Variable expenses (bills that have different amount month by month and include items like: credit cards, water bill, cell phone, etc.). Other variable expenses include entertainment, clothes, groceries, parking, hobbies, and dining out. Because variables expenses include some items that satisfy a want or pleasure, you can reduce this monthly amount by only spending on the necessities of life.

Balance Checkbook

Collect your last 2-3 months of checking/savings account bank statements. Match all transactions with fixed and variable expenses on your budget. Now, you're really starting to budget your money. In addition, add to your budget seasonal expenses like Christmas, birthdays, or anniversaries. Create another savings account and each month put small amounts of money in this account until you reach the funding goal for seasonal expenses.

Expenses Compared To Income

Now, you're ready to compare expenses to income. In a budget, spending and saving are planned based on a written document that has all your income and expenses. Matching every dollar of income with an expense is called zero-dollar budget. Whenever, the budget amounts do not match, you have to make adjustments with expenses or savings. Sometimes, if you have more expenses than income, the first thing you do is reduce variable expenses that are not important. Also, if you have some money remaining after paying all expenses, you can move that amount toward debt reduction for fixed expenses or add it to your savings account. Any overtime or increase in income can be used to reduce fixed or variable expenses.

Track Your Expenses

The best way to track your expenses is to keep receipts and mark on the receipts if the items are fixed and variable expenses. Also, write down expenses and bills paid in the checking account ledger. Keep the ledger updated with expenses, checks written, transfers, and deposits. The main objective of your budget is for you to avoid overspending so you can have money left over after all monthly expenses to save or reduce your debt. Then you can incorporate the envelope system which I will talk about later in this chapter.

Budget Adjustments

Your budget is meant to be adjusted until you better manage your finances. Emergency funds categories must be added because you may have a medical issue, car repair, home maintenance, etc. You're in control of your budget. You have the power to allocate certain money to go to a certain category differently every month. The main focus is making sure all your expenses are paid the correct amount on time. Prepare yourself for unexpected expenses by having more than one savings account so you can transfer money if needed. As your budget changes monthly, hopefully your debt is reduced and you have accumulated a good amount in savings.

2. Pay Bills Before Time

Next, pay all your bills before they are due, especially fixed expenses that have attached interest to it. When you pay these bills before the due date, you are reducing the per day interest charges because total balance is lower. In addition, you are guaranteed to not have any late fees.

3. Sow Money

It is always better to give than receive. God gave you good health, a great family, and job. Sow 10% of your income to show God thanks through your church and other charities to be a blessing. Look for people to sow into, especially if you want people to support or invest in you. You can reap blessings when you sow blessings. Your financial blessings and miracles are attached to you sowing bountifully.

4. First Pay Yourself

Paying yourself is a must for financial independence. It also gives you an emotional lift to have more confidence in your financial future. It is crucial to your happiness and peace of mind to "pay yourself first". God put you as the head of your finances, so yes I want you to imagine writing yourself a check for a ridiculous amount. Even though, technically you are not writing a check. "Pay yourself first" means you're setting aside money for current and future savings like bank savings, emergency funds, 401K, or Roth IRA. Also, "pay yourself first" can pay off debts, credit cards, and student loans. "Paying yourself first" encourages the average person to save money and pay off debts. Typically, "paying yourself first" is around about 10% of your gross income. With "paying yourself first" it encourages a habit of good money management and saving for the future. You "pay yourself first" is rewarding yourself for staying true to your budget.

5. Envelope System

To set up an envelope system is very easy. You get regular mailing envelopes and label each envelope with a variable expense like: groceries, dining out, movies, gas for car, clothes, entertainment, etc. Use your budget to determine the amount you put inside the envelopes. This allows you to not overspend and stay within your budget. It crucial that you only spend what is in the envelopes and not borrow any money from other envelopes. If you have money left over at the end of a pay period, it is best to pay it toward a fixed bill like credit cards or put it in a savings account.

6. Avoid Credit Cards

Next, stop using credit cards. It stops today. Instead of using credit cards, use cash. Cash is king in the financial world. Benefits of not using credit cards primarily make it almost impossible to get in debt. You avoid the temptation of spending money you do not have in your budget. If you carry a balance on a credit card, you end up paying for interest rates, which makes the credit card companies successful and reduces your financial security.

Avoid Credit Cards

CHARGE	USE CREDIT CARD	BENEFITS OF NO CREDIT CARD
Interest	2017 national interest rate average for credits cards is 16.05%(www.creditcards.com). Interest added to balance.	Save on average 16.05% of interest charges.
Annual Fee	Some credit cards charge annual fees of $25 - $99 per year.	Save $25-$99 on annual charges.
Food	Get in debt for perishable items (food) that can be put into a budget.	Use coupons and save up to $1,000 per year.
Entertainment	Using credit card to pay retail price for entertainment.	Pay cash, use groupons/phone apps to save $300 per year.
Gas	Using credit card 1 or 2 times a week to fuel car.	Gas in budget & find the most economical fuel.
Bills	Living above your means and use credit card to pay bills	Remove bills & debt.*Remove cable bill, save over $900 a year.*
Personal Development	Credit cards pay for seminars or books that you never use.	Personal development budget item.
Clothing	Overspending on items you never wear and get into debt.	Savings: apps & newspapers.

The Momentum of Success Technique

WHEN TO USE A
CREDIT CARD

REASON   BENEFITS

REASON	BENEFITS
Building Credit	Report to all three major credit bureaus to improve your credit score. *Pay off entire balance before 25 days to avoid interest/debt.*
Hotel Reservation	Secures reservation; protected by credit cards to dispute any unwanted charges. *Include cost in budget and use debit card/cash to complete transaction.*
Car Rental	Secures rental; credit cards give some kind of car rental coverage in case of an accident. *Include cost in budget and use debit card/cash to complete transaction.*

7. Ask Money Questions

Ask yourself questions before you spend money or make a financial decision. Please, no unexpected spending.

Below are five questions you can ask yourself before you spend money:

1. **Does this purchase satisfy a need or want?**

   Is this purchase something that solves a problem in my life or makes something easier? If I already have this item, do I really need more than one of them? Don't purchase the item just because it is on sale; don't let this be the only reason you purchase. This purchase must satisfy a need and you must regularly use it to get your money's worth.

2. **Can I find this item cheaper?**

   Sometimes you can find the same item at another store. If the item does not have to be new, you can shop for a cheaper price on used items at online shopping stores like: Amazon, eBay, or Overstock. Just factor in the shipping cost in your price comparison. For groceries, purchase a Sunday newspaper or go to online coupon sites to get great savings. Shop around first before purchasing to get the right item for the best price.

3. **Is this purchase within my budget?**
    Don't try to keep up with other people.
    Stay within your budget of fixed and
    variable expenses. Luxury items are not
    included in your budget because they
    come against debt freedom or
    accumulation of savings. Before you can
    purchase this item, it has to be included in
    your budget.

4. **Why am I buying these items?**
    Stick to your budget and do not impulse
    buy or purchase items on an emotional
    whim. Think before you purchase an
    item. List the pros and cons of the
    purchase. If the cons are more than the
    pros, do not purchase the item.

5. **Can I purchase this item later?**
    Delay the purchase for a month or two.
    If this purchase is an important need then
    add it to your budget. Start saving for
    this item every pay period until you have
    enough saved up. Before the final
    purchase, shop around for lower prices.
    Ask yourself if the purchase is a need or
    want. Only purchase items that are on
    sale, you've properly saved up for it, and
    it satisfies a need.

8. Have Fun With Your Money

Use your income and savings to have fun. Whether it is going to a movie, a play, or vacation you have earned the right to have fun because you worked hard & smart for it. Going to the movies, eating at your favorite restaurant, purchasing concert tickets, buying a new book or investing in your personal development are examples. Listed below are 10 ways to have fun spending your money.

1. Pay 1 extra mortgage payment yearly. Save 5 plus years of interest charges on the loan (yes, this is fun!).
2. Become a member of an investment club. Make profits from your money saved.
3. Invest in children. Start an account for children's education or future business.
4. Invent something. Create something that can change the world. Just dream big and solve a problem with your invention.
5. Join a vacation club. Save money and travel the world with your family and friends.
6. Give money to charities. Find a charity that you love and bless them. It feels great to sow.
7. Buy a vacation home. Plan a getaway to a beach and relax.
8. Do home improvements. Build a playground for your kids or remodel your bathroom.
9. Start a business. Make extra money with your creative ideas.

10. Go back to school. Enroll for a college degree or get training for your purpose.

9. Couponing

Use coupons to save money on a weekly basis. You can purchase a Sunday newspaper for $2 and get over $150 worth of coupons for groceries and household items. In addition, you subscribe to online coupons being emailed to you from *coupons.com* or *retailmenot.com*. Your cell phone has coupon apps like *ibotta*. With a low investment, you can save well over $1,000 per year with coupons. Start couponing so you can work on paying off your debts.

With these nine disciplines you can receive more dollars. The policy for your prosperity is to have discipline in your finances. Budgeting before you spend helps you save money in the end. Continue to sow money to other people so blessings continue to come to you. Always reward yourself by paying yourself first. Save tons of interest by paying your bills before they are due. Ask questions before you spend money to make sure it is a need and not a want. You have a strict policy to never use credit cards. Use the envelope system to avoid overspending. Find creative ways to have fun with your money instead of just paying bills. Invest in couponing to save over $1,000 year. You now have financial discipline. You have prosperity. Your dollars are working to make you debt free. You now know how to manage your money better. Go enjoy life! Have fun with your money.

Your Work Is Your Worth

What are you worth? Let's look at your paycheck or W-2 form. Is your paycheck what you're worth? If the compensation is not correct, my question is what are you going to do about it? And what can you do about it? You can work on your worth; that is what you can do about it. Your work must match your worth. Your work must match your paycheck. Your work must match your salary. Your work must match your income. Your income is in your work. What are you going to do about it? You want a promotion; you want increase in your finances, then work on your worth. Become dedicated, become committed, become teachable, and become trainable, in order to work on your worth.

Labor To Add Value

Always seek knowledge by improving with self development training. This increases your worth. When you go to work everyday, try your best to gain an advantage over your coworkers; it's friendly competition, where you're always striving to be better than the next person. You can do it. Your work must match your worth for income. Your work must match your worth for promotion. Your work must match your worth for salary increase, promotion, and a new job title. You can do this. Labor hard and work smart. Be committed and dedicated. Sacrifice by going the extra mile. Clock-in at work early and stay later than others. Be a helping hand on your job. Be a person of influence on your job. Help your manager make key company decisions. Add some value to the company. Even sometimes volunteer to train other employees. Step your game up! Perform your job duties at an all time high! Do something different. Renew your mind. Speak up about your concerns and issues with professionalism. Add value to the company by increasing your worth. Work harder to increase your worth. Get training and development to increase your worth.

You're The Product

More importantly, produce a product that is powerful, impactful and influential. That product is you! You're the greatest product. Your product should be of great value to any company. Therefore, your worth goes up. Be a person of character and integrity. Be trustworthy. Be available to open the store and close the store. Be able to be trusted with people's children. Be trusted with the company's vision and do your best. You're the product that consists of being trustworthy, dedicated, dependable, and loyal.

Your Work = Your Worth

Your Common Sense =
Unlimited Wealth

Common Sense = GRIND your Dream daily.

Common Sense = WORK SMART for
Money.

Common Sense = TITHE 10% of
income to church/charity.

Common Sense = PAYOFF all Debt.

Common Sense = SAVE 10% of income.

Common Sense = INVEST in
Personal Development.

Common Sense = LIVE within
your means.

Common Sense = SELL items you
no longer need.

Common Sense = PURCHASE
Life Insurance.

Common Sense = FILE tax returns with
correct deductions.

Common Sense = MARKET your business
                    for free on social media.

Common Sense = TAKE your lunch to work.

Common Sense = CLIP coupons for savings.

Common Sense = ASK QUESTIONS before
                    you spend money.

Common Sense = MULTIPLE STREAMS
                    OF INCOME is a must.

Common Sense = CASH is King
                    over credit cards.

Common Sense = BUDGET your
                    money wisely.

Common Sense = START A BUSINESS
                    while working a 9-5 job.

Common Sense = SOW MONEY into other
                    people's dream.

Common Sense = PAY ALL BILLS on time.

Common Sense = SAVE $1 A DAY from 1st
job to now to amass at least a $10,000 savings.

Common Sense = PAY EXTRA on mortgage
payments to save years of interest charges.

Common Sense = PAY BALANCE of credit
card off by 30 days to avoid interest charges.

Discipline = Dollars

You want to be wealthy, prosperous, and debt free, but do you have financial discipline? Fill in the blanks below to discover financial discipline statements.

Fun Bless Budget Yourself Save 10% Avoid Invest

To understand how much money you're spending or saving, you must create a _____. This allows you to see everything concerning your finances.

God has been so good to you, and you must return _____ of your income to God.

You have worked hard to earn your income. After tithing, it is important that you pay _____ first.

By any means necessary, _____ credit card debt.

_____ some money for a rainy day fund.

Enjoy your money and spend it on having _____ sometimes.

_____ other people with random acts of kindness.

_____ in well-researched companies
to watch your money grow.

Affirmation Instructions:

Write- Record Daily Affirmations on *3* pieces of paper or index cards (Place at home, car, and work)

State- Speak with a powerful tone and total belief *3* times a day: Morning, Evening, and Before bed.

Meditate- Think about affirmations at least *8* times (exercising, walking, driving, eating, working, etc.).

*14 interactions with the Daily Affirmations = a person's average of 450,000 daily thoughts.

Money Management Affirmations

Monday

I am a great manager in all areas of my finances.

In all areas of my finances, I am a great manager.

My finances are managed great in all areas.

Affirmation Instructions:

Write- Record Daily Affirmations on *3* pieces of paper or index cards (Place at home, car, and work)

State- Speak with a powerful tone and total belief *3* times a day: Morning, Evening, and Before bed.

Meditate- Think about affirmations at least *8* times (exercising, walking, driving, eating, working, etc.).

*14 interactions with the Daily Affirmations = a person's average of 450,000 daily thoughts.

Money Management Affirmations

Tuesday

Consistently, I pay myself first from
my income.
Consistently, when I get income
I pay myself first.
With my income, I consistently
pay myself first.

Affirmation Instructions:

Write- Record Daily Affirmations on 3 pieces of paper or index cards (Place at home, car, and work)

State- Speak with a powerful tone and total belief 3 times a day: Morning, Evening, and Before bed.

Meditate- Think about affirmations at least 8 times (exercising, walking, driving, eating, working, etc.).

*14 interactions with the Daily Affirmations = a person's average of 450,000 daily thoughts.

Money Management Affirmations

Wednesday

God automatically gets 10% of
my money.

10% of my money automatically goes
to God.

I automatically return to God 10% of
my money.

Affirmation Instructions:

Write- Record Daily Affirmations on *3* pieces of paper or index cards (Place at home, car, and work)

State- Speak with a powerful tone and total belief *3* times a day: Morning, Evening, and Before bed.

Meditate- Think about affirmations at least *8* times (exercising, walking, driving, eating, working, etc.).

*14 interactions with the Daily Affirmations = a person's average of 450,000 daily thoughts.

Money Management Affirmations

Thursday

Paying in cash eliminates the use of credit cards.

Credit card usage is eliminated with cash purchases.

The use of credit cards is eliminated by paying with cash.

Affirmation Instructions:

Write- Record Daily Affirmations on *3* pieces of paper or index cards (Place at home, car, and work)

State- Speak with a powerful tone and total belief *3* times a day: Morning, Evening, and Before bed.

Meditate- Think about affirmations at least *8* times (exercising, walking, driving, eating, working, etc.).

*14 interactions with the Daily Affirmations = a person's average of 450,000 daily thoughts.

Money Management Affirmations

Friday

Investing in my purpose has great
return on my potential.
My potential happens because I invest
in my purpose.
There is great return on my potential
by investing in my purpose.

Affirmation Instructions:

Write- Record Daily Affirmations on *3* pieces of paper or index cards (Place at home, car, and work)

State- Speak with a powerful tone and total belief *3* times a day: Morning, Evening, and Before bed.

Meditate- Think about affirmations at least *8* times (exercising, walking, driving, eating, working, etc.).

*14 interactions with the Daily Affirmations = a person's average of 450,000 daily thoughts.

Money Management Affirmations

Saturday

Prosperity is drawn to me because I
save, invest, profit, and share.
When I save, invest, profit, and share I
experience prosperity.
Saving, investing, profiting, and sharing
bring prosperity to me.

Affirmation Instructions:

Write- Record Daily Affirmations on *3* pieces of paper or index cards (Place at home, car, and work)

State- Speak with a powerful tone and total belief *3* times a day: Morning, Evening, and Before bed.

Meditate- Think about affirmations at least *8* times (exercising, walking, driving, eating, working, etc.).

*14 interactions with the Daily Affirmations = a person's average of 450,000 daily thoughts.

Money Management Affirmations

Sunday

My goals are Multiple Streams of
Income and Debt Freedom.
Multiple Streams of Income and Debt
Freedom are my goals.
My goal of Debt Freedom happens
with Multiple Streams of Income.

ABOUT THE AUTHOR

Shawn Momon is known by all social media outlets as "Mr. Affirmation", because of his life changing collection of over 1,000 affirmations and 500 acronyms. He is a catalyst for positive change, where he helps people with career management, and business & personal development through seminars, training programs, and one-on-one coaching.

In addition, he is the author of the upcoming book *The Affirmations of Prosperity*, which he has affirmed to be a New York Times best seller, and to be translated into more than twenty-five languages. He resides in Griffin, Georgia with his wife Anika, and their two children, David and Hannah. Currently serving as the Dean of Student Affairs at New Horizons New Directions Preparatory Academy, Shawn has a major impact on the faculty and students. Follow him on Facebook at Facebook.com/mr.affirmation, Twitter @mraffirmation, and on Instagram @mr_affirmation.

Mindset

Opportunity

Motivation

Enthusiasm

Network

Time Management

Uniqueness

Money Management

M.O.M.E.N.T.U.M.

www.ingramcontent.com/pod-product-compliance
Lightning Source LLC
Chambersburg PA
CBHW022022090426
42739CB00006BA/251